How To Do Your Own Divorce

How To Do Your Own Divorce

A step-by-step guide

Jeremy Rosenblatt

with a foreword by
Lynn Faulds Wood

VERMILION
London

FOR MY MOTHER AND MY FATHER
RUTH AND ELLIOT ROSENBLATT
WITH LOVE

First published in 1993 by Vermilion
an imprint of Ebury Press
Random House
20 Vauxhall Bridge Road
London SW1V 2SA

Second edition revised and updated 1995

Catalogue record for this book is available
from the British Library.

ISBN 0 09 180669 0

Cover design by Patrick McCreeth
Cover illustration by Christopher Brown

Typeset in Palatino
by Hope Services (Abingdon) Ltd
Printed and bound by Mackays of Chatham PLC, Chatham Kent.

Contents

About the Author

Jeremy Rosenblatt read law at the London School of Economics before working as a Research Assistant in the House of Commons. He is the winner of an Anglo-Dutch Cultural Scholarship to the Asser Institute of International Law in The Hague and a Guggenheim Travel Scholarship to Venice. He is a sometime contributor to television and radio as well as being a trained Therapy Counsellor (Lincoln Centre of Psychotherapy). He is the co-author of *International Child Abduction* and the author of *International Adoption* (Sweet and Maxwell). Jeremy Rosenblatt is a barrister specialising in Family Law, living and working in London.

Acknowledgements

The enclosed forms are acknowledged as copyright reproduced with the permission of the Controller of Her Majesty's Stationery Office.

The forms on pages 89, 91, 93, 95, 103, 111, 116 and 119 are reproduced with the permission of The Solicitors' Stationery Society Limited.

Foreword

Whether you are someone who would prefer to represent yourself in court, or who – as is sadly increasingly the case – isn't eligible for legal aid and can't afford the services of a lawyer, *How To Do Your Own Divorce* offers essential information in the conduct of divorce proceedings through the courts of England and Wales.

Concise and informative, it shows you how straightforward most divorces are and tells you everything you need to know – even if you only feel confident enough to represent yourself at the beginning of the legal process. It may be that in the course of proceedings you decide you want to involve a solicitor, but whatever you opt for the real importance of this book is that it offers you the choice.

Lynn Faulds Wood
1993

Introduction

Britain has the highest marriage rate of any country in the EU. It also has the highest proportion of single parents and the highest divorce rate: an astonishing 40 per cent of marriages in Britain end in divorce. The reasons, in descending order of frequency, are:

- money, or the lack of it
- alcohol- and drug-related problems
- extra-marital relationships

Of these, money problems are by far the most common cause of a marriage breaking up. When one or other partner loses their job – a situation that occurs all too often during an economic recession – the couple often find themselves in unexpected financial difficulties. As a consequence, unbearable strains are put on the relationship.

If the partners are owner-occupiers they may not be able to meet their mortgage repayments. But selling up and moving elsewhere cheaper is not always possible when the property market is at a low ebb, and the building society may simply have to repossess their home. Without an income, pension contributions will no longer be made, and any capital saved in bank or building society accounts will rapidly dwindle. From a situation of relative comfort the couple may find themselves in the unfamiliar and frightening position of depending on the state for unemployment benefit and income support. If there are children the economic strain will be intensified because there are more mouths to feed, and what little money is available has to be stretched even further.

It is against this kind of background that people's feelings for one another disintegrate. If the situation becomes serious, the marriage itself is likely to fall apart.

At this stage, divorce is not the only legal option. Judicial separation (formerly known as legal separation: see p. 30) enables the partners to be separated in the eyes of the law without actually being divorced.

Divorce is a traumatic time for everyone concerned. The aim of *How To Do Your Own Divorce* is to offer legal assistance to husbands and wives whose marriages have irretrievably broken down, and in particular to show them how to conduct their own divorce in the courts of England and Wales without going to the expense of a lawyer (the law in Scotland is different, and it is not possible to go into the Scottish system in a short book such as this). Intended as a practical guide through the potential minefield of a divorce, it does not discuss emotional issues: these are amply catered for by a large number of excellent organisations whose names and addresses are listed on p. 68.

The different stages of a divorce case are clearly defined, and the legal terminology – which can be baffling and off-putting to the general public – is carefully explained so that the various terms will be familiar when you encounter them in court. The first stage, petitioning for divorce, is quite straightforward. It involves filling out pre-printed forms, then ensuring that the other party receives them before delivering them to court and going on to the pronouncements of decree nisi and decree absolute. Instructing a solicitor to do this on your behalf might cost about £300 – a worthwhile saving at what may already be a difficult financial time.

The subsequent stages of a divorce, involving the division of the couple's money and property and the future of any children of the marriage, are unfortunately more complicated. Users of this book might therefore feel confident enough to represent themselves at the beginning, but not at later stages. If, however, you do decide to tackle the financial stages yourself but find the process more complicated than you had realised, contact a solicitor and ask him or her to take over. There is little point in trying to save yourself money if you end up making a bad job of it. Remember, you may be eligible for legal aid (see p. 70 for further information on lawyers, costs and legal aid).

Beginning on p. 84 you will find samples of a number of legal forms relating to divorce. No one enjoys filling in forms, especially when they are long and full of technicalities. But while some of these documents might appear complex at first, if you read through them carefully you will see that all they want you to do is to give as much detail as possible regarding your particular application. The aim is to help you, the other side, and the court – there is no ulterior motive. At the end of the day the more honest you are in filling out these forms and providing the information asked for, the quicker the entire process will be and the sooner you can start getting on with the rest of your life.

1

Before You Decide to Get Divorced

If you have got to the point where you or your partner, or both of you, feel that your marriage is no longer viable and you want to get divorced, the law allows you to do so under certain conditions laid down by the Matrimonial Causes Act 1973.

After not less than one year of marriage a petition for divorce – the document that begins the whole process – may be presented to a court by either partner in a marriage that has broken down irretrievably. There are five legally accept-able reasons for a marriage to have reached this stage:

- adultery and unreasonable behaviour
- unacceptable behaviour
- desertion for a continuous two-year period
- two years' continuous separation with the respondent's consent
- five years' continuous separation with or without the respondent's consent

Before a divorce can be considered, you must satisfy the court that at least one of these is true in your case.

Adultery and Unreasonable Behaviour

In legal terms adultery means voluntary sexual intercourse between two members of the opposite sex, one or both of whom are married, though not to each other. If the adultery is admitted it is much easier to prove the grounds for divorce; if it is not, witnesses may be required.

If, after the allegation of adultery, the husband or wife resume living together for a period of six months in total, the adultery will not be regarded as a ground for divorce (this is called the six-month cohabitation rule). It does not matter how long ago the adultery took place as long as the parties have not gone back to live with each other for six months altogether – though four or five months would be acceptable.

But it is not enough just to satisfy these conditions and prove adultery. The petitioner (the person bringing the petition for divorce) must also show that to continue living with the respondent (the partner on whom the petition is served) would create an intolerable situation.

The test is a subjective one: it might not be intolerable for everybody, but as long as the petitioner states it is intolerable that is enough. Nor does the state of intolerability have to stem from the proven adultery – it might arise from a whole host of other things.

Unreasonable Behaviour

In legal terms, this means that the respondent has behaved in such a way that the petitioner cannot reasonably be expected to live with the respondent. Examples of such behaviour patterns include:

- physical violence
- alcohol or drug abuse
- psychological distress
- growing apart
- arguments
- lack of, or too much, sexual intercourse

The six-month cohabitation rule (see above) applies here too.

Desertion

This means that the respondent has left the petitioner for a continuous period of at least two years immediately before the presentation of the petition. No allegation of misconduct is necessary for a divorce to be granted on grounds of desertion, but the court does have to be satisfied on four matters:

- The fact of separation. It may be enough for the parties still to occupy the same home if they live separately within it and do not communicate with each other
- An intention to desert (one partner leaves the other, with no intention of returning), which in itself brings the cohabitation to its end
- That separation was without consent. (The fact that the deserted partner is delighted will not unduly affect the concept of desertion as a ground for divorce)
- That one partner did not have a good reason for living apart from the other, such as needing to take a job in another country

Any period of cohabitation cannot be included in the two-year desertion period – it has to be consistently uninterrupted.

Two Years' Separation and Respondent's Consent

The husband and wife must have lived apart for a continuous period of at least two years immediately before the presentation of the petition, and the respondent must consent to a decree being granted. Again, there need be no allegation of misconduct. The parties can still live under the same roof as long as they are not living as 'husband and wife'.

Either the husband or the wife must have considered the marriage to be at its end throughout the two-year separation period. The partner who is relying on this ground must state the date when this conclusion was reached, and the circumstances. The respondent must give his or her signed consent regarding the fact of separation relied upon by the petitioner.

Five Years' Separation

The husband and wife must have lived apart for a continuous period of at least five years immediately before the presentation of the petition. The respondent's consent is unnecessary.

In legal terminology, the consistency of the separation period and the consideration by one party that the marriage was at its end must be shown. In other words, one of the partners can suggest when it ended and the other can agree; if they do not agree, the divorce might be defended on this issue.

There is also a special defence which can be used against the ground of five years' separation. If the respondent can claim that the divorce would cause him or her grave financial or other hardship, the petition can be opposed. The hardship must be shown to be a consequence of the actual dissolution of the marriage, and not just of its breakdown.

Reconciliation and Therapy

The British are reluctant to look too closely at themselves as individuals because this is regarded as unhealthy self-obsession. In Catholic countries people tend to be more open emotionally and they have the additional outlet of confession to a priest, while America abounds with therapists of all kinds and no one need ever keep their problems to themselves. But on the whole the British have no such safety valve, and traditional social values demand that we keep a stiff upper lip and suffer in silence. Unfortunately this situation only serves to create an atmosphere of simmering tension which may at some stage boil over, possibly into a demand for divorce.

One reason why a marriage might not be working is that one partner has a problem which he or she has not addressed or even necessarily identified. During the course of the marriage problems originating in childhood may surface and reveal themselves in the shape of, say, alcoholism or drug abuse. The argument that such addictions have become evident because of the other partner's attitude does not always hold water. Often these behaviour traits have been there in some form all the time, irrespective of the existence of the partner or of the marriage itself. In such a situation the partner with the problem should make every effort to seek professional help, rather than destroy the marriage because of something within himself or herself as an individual.

Much weight is attached by the courts to what is known as reconciliation between the parties prior to divorce, and whilst that is to be applauded not enough consideration is given to the needs of the individual alone as opposed to those of the husband and wife together. Such needs can be met by therapy in all forms from straightforward counselling to psychotherapy. To help you choose the one that best suits your needs you could discuss the matter with your GP in the first instance. Notice boards in court waiting areas advertise a range of therapy centres, and the organisations listed on p. 68 may also be of assistance.

Only when you have taken steps to deal with any problems within yourself as an individual should you consider attempting the next stage – reconciliation between the two parties to the potential divorce.

Reconciliation Before Divorce

If both parties are going to be legally represented, what is called a certificate of reconciliation must be filed at the court along with the divorce petition. This certificate states whether you have received advice about reconciliation.

During the preliminary stages of the hearing you can have what are called conciliation appointments at court, when you can ask questions of a conciliation officer appointed by the court. Often relationships are saved and marriages remain intact all because of a thirty-minute session which allows the officer to mediate and prevent a couple's anger running out of control.

Where lengthier conciliation is thought appropriate, organisations such as RELATE (formerly the Marriage Guidance Council) provide excellent services to enable the husband and wife to sift through the main areas of disagreement. The court system is experienced at pointing people in the right direction for advice of this kind.

Before considering the legal procedure of petitioning for divorce, the steps described above must be given due attention – which means more than mere lip-service.

Your Legal Rights

When you or your children have been the victim of domestic cruelty of one kind or another, you may want to throw your partner out of the family home. But until you are divorced you have no automatic legal right to do so. If you change the locks, for instance, your partner can obtain a court order enabling him to get back into the home. What you must do in this situation is go to the court to obtain an injunction, known as an exclusion order, to prevent him from entering; only then are you at liberty to change the locks.

If you have suffered anything from harassment to actual violence you may want to obtain another kind of injunction. The purpose of a non-molestation injunction, also known as a personal protection order, is to stop your partner interfering with you or your children. If you have not yet initiated divorce proceedings, you apply to the magistrates' court for a non-molestation injunction; if you have set the ball rolling, or are about to, the divorce court can give you a personal protection order. In the event that your partner fails to comply with either of these two injunctions he can be sent to prison.

The list of organisations on p. 68 includes several which can help in such circumstances.

2
Maintenance Before Divorce Proceedings Are Begun

Money is involved at all stages in a divorce. For simplicity, it can be divided into:

- maintenance before divorce proceedings are initiated (which is what this chapter is about)
- the costs of the actual divorce (see p. 27)
- maintenance arrangements while the divorce is going on, which is known as maintenance pending suit (see Chapter 5)
- the division of the divorcing couple's assets (see Chapter 6)
- permanent maintenance arrangements (see Chapter 6)

Maintenance Orders

Before you petition for either divorce or a judicial separation, you can apply to the family proceedings court (formerly magistrates' court) for an order for financial provision if your partner is not supporting you properly. The Domestic Proceedings and Magistrates' Courts Act 1978 allows either party of the marriage to seek an order where there has been:

- failure to provide reasonable maintenance. The court will consider the wife's needs, obligations and responsibilities in relation to her income, earning capacity and resources, as well as the husband's ability to pay. The wife should show that the husband has been difficult about making money available – for instance that he has made only a few payments or none at all, or that, while pleading impoverishment, he has been seen eating in expensive restaurants and has gone on holiday

- unreasonable behaviour. The court will consider whether the husband has behaved in such a way (drunkenness, say, or physical violence) that it would be unreasonable to expect the wife to continue living with him
- desertion by the husband of the wife who is applying for the order. After hearing what the wife has to say, the court will consider whether desertion can be proved sufficiently as a ground to bring the money application

If the ground is proven, the court can go on to order either periodical payments, or a lump sum payment, to the wife. There is a limit on what the family proceedings court can award. However a consent order, which is based on an agreement between the two partners, has no ceiling.

A periodical payments order can be made under section 7 of the Domestic Proceedings and Magistrates' Court Act 1978:

- if the parties have been living continuously apart for more than three months though not in a state of desertion, or
- if the other party has been making periodical payments to the applicant.

The applicant should specify the total amount of money already received in the three months before she made the application. If the amount ordered would have been less under section 2 of the Act, then the court must order an amount at that level and not under section 7. Once more the court will consider the needs of the parties, the standard of living enjoyed before separation and so on.

An order cannot be backdated to before the date of the application (though a lump sum order can be made to augment the maintenance money), nor can it go on beyond the death of either party. (If the two parties subsequently divorce, the order will come to its end if the party receiving payment remarries.)

Under section 19 of the Act an interim maintenance order can be made. It remains in force for three months, but can be renewed for another three months; it will cease when a final order is made. It is not possible to appeal against an interim order.

How to Apply

The family proceedings court has jurisdiction if at the time of the application:

- both parties reside in England or Wales, or
- the respondent resides in Scotland or Northern Ireland and the parties last resided as man and wife in England or Wales

The court can hear an application to revoke or vary an order (see p. 20) even though one party resides outside England or Wales. The application should be made in the court covering the area where the parties last resided.

Applications, whether for ordinary periodical payments or for a consent order, should be made on standard court forms. State the grounds upon which the application is based – that the family needs money because there is insufficient income coming in and the father, for example, can well afford to make a reasonable payment.

Once the court receives the application it will notify the respondent. The Clerk of the Justices usually decides what evidence is to be heard, and when; the applicant should simply follow his instructions.

The court will ask for a statement of means, giving full details of the financial circumstances of the applicant. The kind of documentary evidence required in court includes such things as:

- pay slips
- P60s
- bank or post office statements
- quarterly bills

This evidence should be shown to the respondent before the couple come to court.

At the hearing, which both applicant and respondent are required to attend, the applicant simply confirms the contents of the financial statement as true, adding anything that has not already been detailed and formally exhibited to the court (called 'handed up to the court').

The applicant will then be cross-examined by the respondent or his legal representative, and the Clerk of the Justices might also have some questions. If the applicant has brought any witnesses who are relevant to her financial situation, they will be called after the applicant's evidence has been given. Then the respondent will give his evidence in reply and the applicant can ask him questions, guided by the Clerk if necessary.

Variation of Orders (see p. 78)

Orders made under sections 2, 6 or 7 of the Domestic Proceedings and Magistrates' Courts Act 1978 can be varied or even revoked by a family proceedings court. Orders for periodical payments and interim orders can be revoked as well. The court can order a lump sum to be paid as a means of varying an order of periodical payments.

In this situation the court will inevitably consider any agreement reached between the parties, as well as the circumstances of the case. Either of the two parties may apply for a variation of the order.

3

From Petition to Decree Absolute

A court in England or Wales (though Scotland and Northern Ireland are different) can grant a decree of:

- divorce
- nullity, or
- separation

These are legal choices available to the divorcing couple for formalising the end of a marriage.

Nullity means that the marriage is ruled never to have been in existence – as, for example, when one partner was pressured into marrying the other. Judicial separation, which some couples use as a 'cooling-off period' while they are deciding whether to get divorced, is dealt with in Chapter 4. Meanwhile this chapter gives a step-by-step account of how to obtain a divorce; financial arrangements during divorce proceedings are discussed in Chapter 5, while information on maintenance after divorce will be found in Chapter 6.

Preparing and Filing the Petition

To initiate divorce proceedings, whichever partner is seeking the divorce (the petitioner) files a petition. This simply means sending two copies of the divorce application to any county court with divorce jurisdiction (see p. 73), or to the Divorce Registry in London (Somerset House, Strand, London WC2R 1LP). The petition must use standard wording and be presented in a particular way as laid down in the Matrimonial Causes Rules 1977 (see p. 84). Forms for this purpose are available from divorce court offices or the Divorce Registry.

A third copy of the petition is required if the reason for divorce is adultery with a named co-respondent. The petitioner must name the co-respondent if an allegation of adultery is being relied upon as the ground for divorce, unless the name and identity of the person involved are unknown; in this situation the petition must state that they are unknown.

Sometimes the petitioner believes that no actual act of adultery has been committed, but wishes to rely for grounds of divorce on what is known as an improper association. This means that the respondent and the third party might, for instance, have had regular intimate dinners together, even though they never had a sexual relationship. In this case the petitioner must make a special application for the court to direct whether this person should become a co-respondent. The application should be made at the directions hearing (see p. 26).

Even if both parties agree to the divorce, it is not possible to file a joint petition – you must decide between yourselves which of you will be cast as petitioner and which as respondent. Your choice of role in this situation is purely a formality and does not usually have any bearing on how the court subsequently deals with children and financial matters.

At the date of the petition, one or other of the parties must have been permanently and consistently resident in England or Wales for a period of one year.

Various other documents must be filed at court at the same time. Briefly (and with certain exceptions), these are:

- marriage certificate
- statement of arrangements for children
- certificate of reconciliation
- a fee is also payable

First, the marriage certificate: if the original is not available (remember, it will not be returned afterwards), an official copy can be obtained from the General Registry of Births, Deaths and Marriages, OPCS Southport, Smedley Hydro, Trafalgar Road, Birkdale, Southport, Merseyside, or from the General Register Office, St Catherine's House, Kingsway, London WC2B 6JP. An ordinary photocopy is not acceptable, and if the certificate is in another language it must be accompanied by an authenticated translation.

You must also present two copies of a completed form

(available from the same sources as the petition form) stating what arrangements are proposed for any children of the two parties. 'Children' in this context (called 'relevant children' on the form) means young people under sixteen, or under eighteen and still undergoing full-time education or training, who are:

- blood children of either the husband or the wife
- legally adopted children
- stepchildren
- any other children if one of the divorcing partners believes that they were brought up by one or other of them within the family itself

Children are often the casualties of divorce, and their interests are therefore rightly regarded by the court as being of paramount importance. The court will want to know about practical arrangements once the divorce is complete: where the children will live, with whom, whether the other parent will be in contact and the frequency of that contact, schooling, general day-to-day care and maintenance. If the divorcing parents cannot agree which of them the child should live with (residency), decree absolute will not be pronounced until this matter is resolved (see Chapter 7).

At this early stage it may not be possible to answer all the questions on the statement of arrangements form, so just give answers where you can. Any previous orders relating to the children or any information to do with the marriage (living abroad, for instance, or the children going to school in another country) should accompany the petition.

If, when the respondent receives his copy of the divorce petition and the accompanying documents, he agrees with the proposed arrangements for the children, he should sign the statement of arrangements form. Alternatively, he can send his own proposals to the court on a form and the court will send a copy to the petitioner.

If the district judge is satisfied with the statement of arrangements for the children, the petitioner will receive a form stating that the court will not have to exercise its powers under the Children Act 1989. However if the judge is not satisfied, the matter will have to go to trial (see Chapter 7).

As mentioned earlier, a divorcing husband or wife acting

on his or her own behalf and not employing a solicitor does not have to include with the petition a certificate of reconciliation (see p. 15). However, it is always sensible to consider the possibility of reconciliation before filing for divorce.

The last page of the petition, known as the prayer, is actually a request to the court for:

- the marriage to be dissolved
- an order for costs (that is, of the divorce itself) to be made against the respondent and/or the co-respondent (there is no obligation to follow this through if for any reason you change your mind)
- ancillary relief (a general application for maintenance:. Remember to claim this now, or you may be barred from doing so later in the proceedings
- any orders in relation to the children

The petition asks for your solicitor's signature. Obviously, if you are conducting your own case you will sign it yourself. A fee (around £40) is payable when the petition is filed. This is waived if the petitioner is in receipt of certain state benefits (income support or family credit), or is participating in what is known as the green form scheme for those on low incomes (see p. 71).

Serving the Petition

Once all these documents have been received by the court, it forwards to the respondent one copy of the petition and one copy of the statement of arrangements for children. Accompanying them are a notice of proceedings and an acknowledgement form; the respondent should sign the latter and return it to the court as proof of service. Where adultery is alleged and the co-respondent has been named on the petition, a copy of the petition and an acknowledgement form are also sent to that person.

What are known as copies of service should be obtained by the court for all parties to the divorce. A copy of service is documentary proof that the other side has been sent the petition: a recorded delivery receipt, for example, would do.

If the acknowledgement of service form is not returned to

the court and the postman has been unable to deliver the documents, the court resorts to personal service. This means that the documents are delivered personally by the bailiff of the county court or a process server; the petitioner will probably have to pay for this. Both bailiff and process server have to provide the court with an affidavit that the respondent or co-respondent has indeed received the documents. (If you wish to save money, it is in fact quite acceptable for anyone over the age of sixteen to carry out personal service of documents, and then to complete an affidavit to say that they have done so.)

Personal service is sometimes necessary where the respondent or co-respondent is trying to avoid receiving the documents and is therefore unlikely to sign for recorded delivery. Where service cannot be achieved, an order for 'substituted service' can be sought: this means that the court will be satisfied by an advertisement in a newspaper, for example.

Undefended Petition

When the respondent receives his copy of the petition, he is invited to show notice of intention to defend the divorce. If he does not do so, or if he does not file an answer which states what he feels about the petition (see p. 87), then the matter will go ahead as an undefended divorce. This is the most commonly encountered kind, and describes a situation in which the respondent does not come forward to prevent the divorce going through. (Defended divorces are discussed on p. 28.)

The petitioner must now swear an affidavit supporting her grounds of divorce. It is filed with the application for the next stage, which is called directions for trial.

There are five standard types of affidavit to choose from, depending upon the ground of divorce relied upon, and the forms can be obtained from the divorce court counter. The petitioner should state quite simply exactly what has happened to bring about the situation in which she is seeking a divorce.

The petitioner must always identify the signature of the respondent if the acknowledgement of service is signed in order to prove service, and this should be attached to the affidavit in support. If the respondent is making admissions relied upon by the petitioner and/or consenting to the divorce he too must sign, making those admissions and/or giving his consent. In matters of adultery, the co-respondent must do likewise.

The petitioner can then apply at the court divorce counter for a directions hearing. This is a hearing before a district judge at which he can order any further information he thinks should be presented. The district judge's aim here is to assist the final hearing for instance, he may issue directions to file evidence in affidavit form within a certain time, so that by the date of the final hearing all the evidence will be available.

If the divorce is thought to be an ordinary one without complications, as most are, it will be put on what is called a special procedure list. An application for directions for trial (see below) and an affidavit of evidence, which must be sworn in front of a witnessing person (there will be someone at the court counter), should be made.

The affidavit must state:

- that the respondent (and co-respondent, where appropriate) have received the petition
- that the respondent and any named person admit to adultery (or else whatever other ground of divorce is relied upon)
- that the respondent consents to divorce where the grounds are living apart for two years and the arrangements for the children are agreed to

Directions for Trial

At this stage, which the petitioner does not have to attend, the district judge considers the petition, the affidavit in support and other documents that are being relied upon. He will then state either his satisfaction or dissatisfaction that the petitioner is entitled to the decree.

Dissatisfaction usually arises where the proper procedures have not been followed or where certain admissions that are required by the court have not been forthcoming. In this event the case may be withdrawn from the special procedure list, or the petitioner may be given a further opportunity to satisfy the court about these grey areas.

Decree Nisi

Once the court is satisfied, a date and time for the pronouncement of a decree nisi by a judge in open court will be supplied. The petitioner, respondent and co-respondent will receive from the court a certificate of entitlement to the decree. Once more, there is no requirement to attend. If there are no children, documentary confirmation will be supplied by the court to the effect that this is indeed so.

Costs

If, in the prayer that forms part of the petition (see p. 24), the petitioner has asked for an order for costs to be made against the respondent and/or co-respondent, the court will now consider this matter, which is entirely at its discretion. If the court consents, the petitioner will be sent a form (referred to as supplementary to decree nisi). Copies will also be sent to the respondent and co-respondent as appropriate.

Decree Absolute

The decree absolute may be delayed if the court is not yet satisfied with the arrangements to be made concerning the children. Therefore the petitioner should make sure that she has received from the court a copy of the document which states that the judge has decided that decree absolute need not be held up for this reason. Once this has been received (or if there are no children) the petitioner can apply for decree absolute, using yet another standard form and paying a fee (about £15) to the court office, as soon as six weeks have elapsed since the decree nisi was pronounced.

Unless, as mentioned earlier, the petitioner is exempt from

paying fees because she is receiving state benefit, a fee is payable when you apply for decree absolute (about £15). Copies of the decree absolute, which must be produced if either of the divorcing partners wishes to get married again, will then be sent by the court to the petitioner, the respondent and, where relevant, the co-respondent.

If there is a delay of more than twelve months between the pronouncing of the decree nisi and the application for decree absolute, a written explanation will be required by the court.

Defended Divorces

Most divorces are not defended – understandably, since it involves a full hearing in court with all the attendant expense of lawyers. People tend to defend petitions if they feel aggrieved about the way the marriage is coming to its end: often the respondent accepts, albeit grudgingly, that the marriage is over but objects to the reasons stated in the petition.

This does not, however, necessarily justify defending a divorce. A divorce should only be defended where the respondent does not believe that the marriage should come to an end. Even so, bear in mind that in a secular, democratic society it is highly unlikely that any court is going to make a petitioner remain in a marriage which she believes to be finished.

If you are a respondent and you wish to defend the divorce, you must say so on the notice of proceedings form, which you will receive from the court along with your copy of the petition. This form must be sent back to the court within eight days of your receiving it.

From the date when you receive the petition you then have twenty-nine days in which to file at court what is known as an answer to the petition (see p. 86) – a refutation, simple or detailed, of the 'facts' as presented in the petition. If no answer is sent to the court within this period, the petitioner can apply for directions for a trial.

The petitioner will herself have to refute whatever defence the respondent makes out, within fourteen days of receiving his answer; this is known as the reply (see p. 87). If she simply wants a divorce as quickly as possible, she might feel there is little point in replying as it will waste more time and increase costs. However, as the trial will consider what the respondent has to say in his answer to the petition, the petitioner may have no choice but to refute what he is alleging in defence.

At the hearing in court, which must be attended by both husband and wife, by their legal representatives if any, and by any witnesses, each side will give evidence. The court then makes its finding, either allowing or disallowing the divorce.

4
Judicial Separation

Judicial separation, as opposed to divorce, is sought for one of two reasons:

- as a stepping stone leading up to a petition for divorce. It is often used where a married couple are still uncertain whether they want the finality of divorce, and so they try a period of official separation instead
- if the two partners acknowledge that the marriage has irretrievably broken down but cannot have a divorce for religious reasons

The following are exactly the same as in divorce:

- the grounds relied upon
- the timing of a petition – it cannot be brought sooner than one year after the date of marriage
- financial relief
- the obtaining of non-molestation orders and exclusion injunctions in the case of domestic violence
- being judicially separated removes any legal obligation to carry on living with a spouse

But unlike in divorce, neither party can be said to have deserted the other. And where wills are concerned, it is as though the marriage was still in force: if one party dies without making a will, the other will inherit a portion of the estate just as if they had still been married.

Deed of Separation

This is a document which is normally drawn up privately in a solicitor's office, and since deeds of separation can be complicated things it is probably best not to attempt to do this yourself. The document will state the grounds for separation and any arrangements that you are making in connection with children, maintenance and expenses. Although the deed is drawn up privately, either party can rely upon it at a later stage if one of them is not complying with its terms – concerning maintenance payment, for example – and they have to go to court.

How to Obtain a Judicial Separation

Getting a judicial separation involves practically the same steps as getting a divorce. As long as the petition passes through undefended, it will appear before the district judge on his special procedure list.

Conciliation features in cases of judicial separation too. It is advisable for the petitioner to make the court aware that conciliation has been considered.

Once the ground is proved, the court grants the decree. Where there are relevant children (see p. 23 for a definition), their position has to be clarified by the court before any decree is granted. A decree of judicial separation will not prevent any subsequent divorce being granted on the same facts.

If one partner objects there will be a trial hearing, which will consist of each side saying its piece and the court then making a decision whether or not to grant the separation. In the main the court is likely to grant the separation.

Unlike in divorce, judicial separation comes into being as soon as it is granted – in other words, there is only one decree. Once you are judicially separated, neither of you can marry again unless and until you get divorced.

Financial Matters

Under a judicial separation you can obtain the same financial provision as if you were divorced (see Chapter 6). If you go on to get divorced and seek financial provision there too, you do not necessarily have to gather and produce any more evidence than what you will have already done as part of the financial hearing on judicial separation.

A husband can still claim the married man's tax allowance even though he is judicially separated. The Inland Revenue rules state that to do so a husband has to live with his wife or at least wholly maintain her. However, the Revenue is fortunately pragmatic and does not usually enforce this rule too rigidly. Of course, spouses often prefer payments to be registered as part of court orders in case payments are not made and then the partner who is paying denies having made any earlier payments. Registration ensures legal recognition and therefore a certain degree of protection.

When a decree of judicial separation is granted, the court may make one of the following financial orders. They cover periodical payments and lump sums, to (or on behalf of) the other partner:

- an order that either party shall make to the other such periodical payments, and for such term, as may be specified in the order
- an order that either party shall make to the other, to the satisfaction of the court, such periodical payments, and for such term, as may be specified
- an order that either party shall pay to the other such lump sum or sums as may be specified
- one partner to pay a lump sum to the other, to enable the other to meet liabilities or expenses reasonably incurred in maintaining himself or herself, before making an application for an order in his or her favour
- the payment of a lump sum, or of instalments in amounts specified in the order; the court may require security against the payment of these instalments

Where a decree nisi had been granted based upon two or five years' separation the court can consider the respondent's financial position as it will be after a divorce. The court cannot make a decree absolute unless it is satisfied that the petitioner will not be expected to make any financial payment to the respondent, or that the financial payment which has been made is reasonable, fair or what is called 'the best that can be made altogether'.

The court will expect either provision to be made before

the granting of decree absolute, or an undertaking and suggested plan on the part of the petitioner.

Where a couple are judicially separated the court cannot make financial or property adjustment orders unless the respondent has applied for them to be made. However, because the court can withhold decree absolute the petitioner is likely to be sensible regarding the disposition of financial assets.

5
Maintenance During Divorce Proceedings

Because the main financial settlement of a divorce is not made until the stage of decree nisi and does not apply until decree absolute, the courts allow you to claim what is called maintenance pending suit (MPS). This refers to periodical payments which can be made to either the petitioner or the respondent, under section S22 of the Matrimonial Causes Act 1973, while the divorce is going on. Children can also receive periodical payments in their own right at this stage under section S23 of the Act.

Maintenance pending suit can be sought at any time after the presentation of the petition, but it makes sense to do so as soon as possible since it may take several weeks before the district judge considers the application and grants any order (though the order can be backdated to the time when the petition was filed). The amount awarded is based on the needs of the person seeking the relief balanced against the ability of the other partner to pay.

This is how you set about obtaining an MPS order:

- obtain an application form from the court office
- from the same source, get an affidavit form on which you will state your means and needs, to be supported by appropriate bills, pay slips and so on
- at a directions hearing the district judge will issue directions about the evidence required
- the other side has to be served with the application, and in response must swear an affidavit declaring his means and needs. If the respondent fails to do so, the judge will force his hand by setting a high amount for the maintenance order

Periodical payments can be paid either weekly or monthly. An MPS order usually terminates when the decree is made absolute – at which time other, long-term means of financial support will be put into effect.

6

Redistributing the Family Finances

Initiating the Long-Term Financial Settlement

As advised in Chapter 2, the application for what is known as ancillary relief is best made in the petition that starts off the whole proceedings (though it is only the petitioner and not the respondent who can do this – see below). Having done so, you should then obtain from the court office the appropriate forms that indicate your intention to proceed with the financial application (they are different for petitioner and respondent). Because of waiting lists in county courts, the notice of application should be filed as soon as possible.

If the application for financial ancillary relief was not made in the petition, leave will have to be granted by the district judge before you can proceed. Leave can be applied for when you give notice that you intend to proceed with the financial application, and the court will then allocate a time for the hearing. Notice of the application must be served on the other side; ordinary post is sufficient for this.

It is sensible for both petitioner and respondent to make any application for financial relief before they receive a decree absolute. No application can be considered if you remarry.

A claim for periodical payments – that is, maintenance money – should also have been made in the petition, as mentioned on p. 17. Periodical payment orders can be backdated to when the petition was filed. They can be given a time limit (though an extension can be applied for) and will in any case cease when the payee dies or remarries. A change in the amount can also be applied for (see p. 21).

Directions

At any time during the proceedings the district judge can make directions about the filing and serving of documents. A date for a directions hearing will be set by the court. Directions are usually no more than plain instructions on what to do next, or on what is expected regarding the transfer of documentary evidence between the parties.

The Family Home and Other Property

In your notice of application you should state what you propose should happen to the former family home. Most petitioners want to have the home transferred into their sole name under what is called a property adjustment order. If it is already in your sole name, the other party may contest this.

Where the property adjustment concerns land, you should state:

- where the land is
- whether the title is a registered one; if so, give the title number (your local Land Registry office, whose address can be obtained from the town hall, will give you the title number)
- whether there is a mortgage attached to it

If the petitioner is seeking a property adjustment order, a copy of the notice of application form must be served on any mortgagee before the district judge will consider the application. Simply write to the building society or bank that is lending the money, advising them of your proposal either to take over the mortgage repayments, if that is the case, or to transfer the house to the petitioner. Their agreement is essential (on this topic, see also Chapter 8).

Stating Your Means to the Court

An affidavit of means is required at this stage, stating the petitioner's financial position in as simple and straightforward a way as possible. It can detail the financial history of the marriage, though what the divorcing couple often do not realise is that, in the main, there is no 'his' or 'hers' or even 'mine' in a marriage; it is all 'ours', and that is why a court has to make the divisions of property unless agreement is reached between the parties themselves.

Very often the courts provide standard forms containing questions on most financial aspects of a marriage, such as mortgage repayments, cars owned, savings, stocks and shares, pension funds, and outgoings in terms of electricity, gas, telephone, water and council tax bills. You do not have to use these forms, but they are a useful guide.

Two copies of the notice of application, together with the affidavit, must be filed with the court. A fee is payable (about £20). The application is officially stamped (this is called sealing) and returned to the petitioner, who must forward it to the respondent, along with a copy of the affidavit, within four days. The respondent is required to file an affidavit in reply within fourteen days.

More often than not, the petitioner has to apply for a hearing because the two parties cannot agree on the division of assets.

Speeding Up a Slow Respondent

If the respondent does not file an affidavit in reply within fourteen days of being served with the notice of application, the petitioner can seek an order from the court that he should do so. If that also fails, the petitioner should go back to court to obtain a further order together with a penal notice (this simply means that if the respondent fails to comply he could be sent to prison unless he can give a good reason for his inaction), and the petitioner should deliver the new documents by personal service (see p. 24).

Courts sometimes use interim orders (see pp. 19 and 20) as a means of making the respondent comply. If the sum set is very high, the respondent will usually file an affidavit – if only to try to prevent the court setting an even higher sum at the main hearing.

Documents and Evidence Required

All documents relating to financial matters must be produced as evidence of means. These would include, where relevant:

- bank statements
- share certificates
- pension policies
- an official valuation of the former family home (normally carried out by an estate agent)

Bank statements usually need to go back to one year before the hearing. Both husband and wife will want to check up on transactions in and out of an account to see if there is anything suspicious. Cash withdrawals, for instance, might indicate that one of the partners is giving someone else money whilst claiming to be impoverished. Cash deposits could mean that one of them has an undisclosed source of income.

Full details of pension policies must be revealed because a petitioning wife, for example, will lose her former husband's pension entitlement once they are divorced. Computations should be obtained from the pension fund managers stating what lump sum and/or income payment the husband would receive on retirement, and what lump sum and/or income payment the wife would have received on the husband's death or on his early retirement.

As the home is often the main asset of the divorcing couple it is essential that both of them should agree on what it is worth. If they cannot agree, at the directions hearing the district judge may ask for one or two valuers to come to court as witnesses, so that he can then choose an appropriate figure. This obviously costs money, so it is always best if the couple can agree the property valuation between them.

Sometimes a witness may be called on to confirm what the divorcing couple say about their financial situation. Ideally, their evidence should first be produced in affidavit form in advance of the hearing (see under Hearing, below).

Showing the Documents to the Other Side

What is known in legal terms as 'discovery of documents' or 'inspection on discovery' (which simply means showing all the documents to the other side) usually takes place fourteen days after the filing of the last affidavit. However it is sometimes inevitable that certain items, such as the valuation of a home, are not produced until the last minute. Do not be put off if the new evidence is difficult to weigh up immediately. If it is served just before a hearing you can apply for an adjournment. The other side can then be ordered to pay your costs if the fault is thought to be theirs.

Forcing the Other Side's Hand

Before the hearing, you can obtain from the court office a copy of a form known as a Rule 2.63 Questionnaire, and use it to ask the respondent whatever you like about financial matters. These questions are a sensible way of cutting down on court time and preventing unnecessary delay through adjournments. If, for instance, you want sight of a particular bank statement or share certificate that has not been shown 'on discovery', simply use the form to ask for it to be produced.

If the questions are not answered, an application for directions should be made so that the district judge can order the disclosure of the information concerned. Once more, in this situation a costs order is likely to be made against the unhelpful respondent.

If a particular witness is required – for example, the respondent's high-earning live-in girlfriend – and the respondent refuses to bring her to court, the petitioner can request her to be summonsed through the ordinary court channels. The counter staff will tell you how to go about this. A subpoena form (a legal requirement to appear in court, willingly or not) can then be sent to the other side. Ordinary post can be used in the first instance; if this fails to produce results, use personal service.

The Court Bundle

This is simply the way the court refers to the sheaf of documents which are being used as evidence – bank statements, share certificates, valuations and so on. The bundle should be provided by the applicant for ancillary relief, and its contents must be agreed in advance between petitioner and respondent. Only original documents are permissible. For reference purposes, husband and wife should each take photocopies of all documents for themselves.

The bundle should be limited to essential documents that either party will need to rely upon in the course of giving evidence, or that have already been referred to in affidavits or questionnaires. The court will not want to cope with a massive bundle unless it is strictly necessary.

If the respondent does not agree to certain documents forming part of the bundle there will have to be two separate bundles, one from the petitioner and the other from the respondent. Once more, this kind of thing takes up extra court time and should be avoided if possible.

The Whole Truth and Nothing but the Truth

When making financial arrangements after divorce, full and frank disclosure is essential. If one partner conceals money or other assets and this is subsequently discovered, a court will come down strongly on him or her when making its order. Similarly, if one former partner finds out years later that the other failed to disclose a sizeable figure, there is nothing to stop the aggrieved party seeking to set aside an earlier, less generous order. In being honest, divorcing couples are assisting the court and, more importantly, themselves.

The Hearing

The petitioner should 'open' the case by simply telling the court the history of the marriage, including relevant dates such as those of the marriage itself, house purchase and the birth of relevant children. She should then refer the district judge to the affidavits relied upon and to the court bundle.

After the petitioner has told the court about her financial state she will be cross-examined by the respondent. The district judge might also have questions to ask her. She can then call any witnesses she chooses to confirm what she has said about her financial situation. If, for instance, the petitioner now has a job which pays less than her previous one, and the respondent does not believe her, a colleague might be produced to confirm her salary.

Any evidence of this sort should first have been put in affidavit form and then served on the other side, although courts do sometimes allow surprise witnesses at the last moment. In this situation the giving of evidence is at the district judge's discretion.

Equal Division of Assets

Short, childless marriages can cause complications: sometimes a straightforward equal division of assets is agreed to, while at other times one party just wishes to repay however much money the other has put into the home. The needs aspect here will be balanced against the entitlement. Where an equal division is in dispute the court might have to hear evidence of what one party has actually contributed, or of the length of time the parties cohabited if they did so before getting married.

What the Court Considers in Questions of Maintenance

Children

The Child Support Agency now deals with child maintenance. If you telephone the Agency's local office they will send you a form requesting information on your financial status and the suspected financial status of the other party from whom you are seeking payment.

Working Wives

The question of whether the ex-wife should earn her living is quite a subjective one, and each case tends to be treated on its own merits. If, for instance, she has not previously had a job and is still looking after young children, the court is unlikely to put her in the position where she has to go out to work; it will, however, probably expect her to do so when all the children have reached school age. Likewise if a woman does not have small children but is over a certain age (say forty) and has never worked, the court will not necessarily expect her to start doing so now.

But in the case of a reasonably young woman unencumbered by pre-school age children, her protestations that she has no experience of the workplace will probably not wash. The least a court will expect her to do is find a clerical job where minimal qualifications are required, or work on the counter in a store. The courts do, however, take the state of the job market and the economy into account.

Other Circumstances to Be Taken into Account

The courts also consider matters such as:

- likely inheritance from an elderly relative with an unmortgaged home
- remarriage and any associated financial gain
- the age of the divorced couple
- the duration of the marriage

If one party has substantially dissipated the family's assets without due reason – through gambling, say, or expensive shopping habits – the court will take this behaviour into account when a final order is made.

Sale and Transfer of Property

The court has the power to order the valuation and sale of any property in which either husband or wife has a beneficial interest, and to select a solicitor to conduct the sale. The order for sale can be made at the same time as orders for secured periodical payments, lump sums or property adjustment; however, it cannot come into effect until decree absolute has been pronounced. The court can dictate how the proceeds of the sale should be divided. If one side fails to sell the home the court can order other assets, say shares, to be sold to compensate the waiting partner if she makes the appropriate application.

If someone else has a share in the former family home (see Chapter 8) they will have the right to be heard, but the court can still order a sale irrespective of the interest of someone who is not a former husband or wife.

The former home can be settled upon one party to the divorce or both. If one partner wishes to buy the other out, the court can order the sale to be postponed to allow the buyer to raise the necessary money. The sale can also be postponed in other circumstances, for example:

- until the youngest child is either eighteen or has ceased full-time education, whichever is later, or
- until one party decides to cohabit with someone else, or
- until one party marries again, or
- until one party dies.

The court will not transfer the former family home to the wife if she cannot afford the mortgage payments, unless the local DSS office has indicated (which it rarely does in advance) that it will make these payments on her behalf.

Property adjustment orders can be made for any children of the family – property can be transferred to the child or even to another person on the child's behalf. Usually these orders relate to the former family home, but they can also relate to property within that home.

Calderbank Letters

Both petitioner and respondent have the right to make what is called a Calderbank offer – an offer in the form of a letter to the other side that cannot be disclosed to the court in the course of a trial. If, for example, the respondent rejects the petitioner's offer and ends up with less on the decision of the court, the Calderbank letter can be produced to show what the petitioner was offering. The question of the respondent paying the petitioner's costs from the date of the Calderbank letter to the date of the hearing can then be considered by the district judge.

Calderbank letters are a complex business, and it is probably not advisable to consider using them without advice from a solicitor.

Consent Orders

Even at the door of the court, there is nothing to stop the two parties negotiating an agreement by consent. If the respondent, for example, now agrees to an offer that the petitioner originally sought but that was initially rejected, this is obviously a good reason to agree.

But the consent order must still be passed by the court because the district judge, having read all the associated affidavits, has a duty to ensure fairness. This is especially so where, for example, a clean break (see p. 46) is being made, as a result of which the petitioner will no longer be seeking periodical payments from the respondent.

The district judge will want to be satisfied that the petitioner has sufficient income to support herself, or that, if she is in a slightly precarious financial position but wants nothing from the respondent, then at least she fully understands what she is doing. Also, wherever there are children the court will ensure that the financial arrangement in any consent order properly reflects their needs, irrespective of any clean break between their parents.

The Clean Break

A clean break allows the two parties to become totally independent of each other. A psychological factor is involved: divorcing couples often feel a need to split completely from each other, and financial dependence can be an unhappy reminder. Most clean breaks, therefore, only take place where there is sufficient money to go round – typically, when there will be enough capital from the sale of the family home to enable both partners to rehouse themselves.

Even if there are insufficient funds at this stage to rehouse both partners, if each is holding down a good job then a clean break can often still be achieved. This is because mortgages can be raised in the knowledge that enough income will be available to make the repayments.

But a clean break is not always sought by the parties to the divorce – sometimes courts impose it because they feel that it is the best thing for the couple in question. Conversely, where a clean break is requested but one party would be financially vulnerable, the court might not allow it.

It is, however, unlikely that a court will impose a clean break where one is resisted, even if on the facts it would be an appropriate order to make. Sometimes, to protect a wife a court might still order the husband to pay maintenance, but only at the notional rate of 1p per annum. Technically this is not a clean break, because it still enables the wife to come back to court if necessary and seek maintenance from the husband.

The only orders allowable in a true clean break situation concern lump sums or property adjustment – the respondent to transfer an amount of money or his share of the former family home. The questions of maintenance and any other applications, including applications under the Inheritance Act 1975 for money from the estate of the other party if they were to die, are dismissed.

If there are children still entitled to financial support (see below), this factor will not preclude a clean break between the parents and will not preclude the respondent, say, from paying maintenance for the children.

Financially, a clean break can mean:

- the wife keeps the house but receives no maintenance
- the husband does not get the house but pays the wife no maintenance
- the husband and wife share the proceeds of the sale of the house, and neither pays the other maintenance

Changing Circumstances

Where a clean break is not ordered, the parties must accept that changing financial circumstances in subsequent years may demand a rethink. If, for instance, the former husband loses his job and is therefore unable to make the maintenance payments originally ordered, the two parties will either have to agree reduced payments or return to court to obtain a legal ruling. In such circumstances it is best for both former spouses to try to be realistic. Reduced maintenance payments may not be very attractive, but going to court to try to force a man to pay what he cannot afford costs money too.

Payments for Children: Lump Sum

An application can be made to the court for a lump sum to be awarded to a parent in order to buy, for example, a bed, a refrigerator or some carpet for a child of the family to make use of. The application is dealt with through the courts and not through the Child Support Agency, and can be made at any stage of the divorce proceedings, or after the divorce, under the Children Act 1989. The court will consider:

- needs
- income
- earning capacity
- property and other financial resources
- resources
- standard of living
- any physical or mental disability
- the manner in which the children were previously educated or trained, and the manner in which the parents expect them to be educated or trained

How to Apply for Maintenance for a Child

The Child Support Act 1991 has removed the ability of one party to apply to the court for maintenance for a child, and therefore also the ability of the court to award maintenance for a child.

As from 5 April 1993 the party will first contact their local Child Support Agency office and then fill in the form which will be sent to them. If the parent with care is working, he or she can still go back to court for the time being if there is an existing maintenance order.

The Child Support Agency came into being particularly to chase absent parents where the parent with care of the children is on Income Support, Family Credit or Disability Working Allowance. The scheme also attracts applications from parents with care of the children, who are working but who nevertheless need or cannot get maintenance from the absent parent, and who do not have an existing court order. The absent parent might send money to the parent with care who is working, for instance, but it might not be enough to support the children. Where there is a disagreement of this kind, the Child Support Agency will make the calculation of what is needed. However, it should be borne in mind that certain local offices will not make calculations until 1996 if there is an existing arrangement, not in the form of a court order, between the parents.

If the parent with care is frightened about divulging information on the absent parent's whereabouts – perhaps because a child was born without the absent parent's knowledge or in the course of an affair – the parent with care can state to the Agency that such information will cause distress. It will then be up to the Agency to decide whether or not to press for the information and seek maintenance from the absent parent.

Considering the Calculation

When making the calculation the following are taken into account:

- the day-to-day costs of maintaining a child

- the incomes of both the parent who has care and the absent parent, taking into consideration tax, national insurance, rental and mortgage expenses, and other children for whom either parent cares or is financially responsible

The Partners of Parents

The partners of either parent will not be expected to pay towards the maintenance of any children who are not theirs.

The Absent Parent

This parent is entitled to contact the Child Support Agency and volunteer financial information before the Agency makes contact.

When the parent with care fills in the form regarding the absent parent, the Agency will try to locate the latter through official Inland Revenue or national insurance records (assuming the address is not already known). Once the address is known, it will only be divulged with the absent parent's agreement. If, once located, the absent parent refuses to cooperate, he will be at risk of receiving a higher maintenance calculation from the Agency.

If the absent parent is receiving Income support, is over eighteen, is fit for work, and has no dependent children living at home, there could be a required calculation of £2.20 a week.

Cost of the Agency

The cost of all this to the Agency is about £44 per annum for assessment and review, and £34 per annum for collection. The parties will be expected to pay unless:

- they or their partner receive Income Support, Family Credit or Disability Working Allowance
- they are under sixteen, or under nineteen and in full-time education up to A-level or the equivalent
- their income falls below certain limits

These are the latest government amendments:

The Government's White Paper, called Improving Child Support, has stated that parents who have care of their children and are in work and not on benefits, will not be taken on by the Child Support Agency until 1996. This puts those parents in a difficult situation, because, unless they have a maintenance order made by the court prior to April 1993, or an application for a maintenance order, made prior to 1993, they will not be able to return to the courts.

The changes to the maintenance formula from April 1995 are:

1. An absent parent will not be assessed to pay more than 30 per cent of normal net income in current child maintenance or more than 33 per cent in current maintenance and areas.
2. A broad-brush adjustment will be a part of the maintenance formula which will take into account previous 'clean break', final, property or capital settlements. They will no longer be ignored.
3. An allowance will be granted for high travel-to-work costs.
4. Housing costs for a new partner or step-parent will be granted.
5. The maximum level of maintenance payable under the formula for high earners will be cut.
6. From April 1997, parents with care on income support or a job-seeker's allowance will be able to build up a 'maintenance credit', up to a maximum amount of £1000, which will be paid back to them from the Treasury when they start working again, for at least sixteen hours per week.

7

Children: Contact and Residency

Young people are children in the eyes of the law until they reach the age of eighteen, and the differences in law between children born within marriage and those born outside have now been mostly eliminated. When a court evaluates a child's future after the parents have divorced, the main consideration will be the child's welfare.

Conflict over Children at the Start of the Divorce

If the petitioner and respondent cannot agree about the statement of arrangements for children when the petition is originally filed, a hearing will have to be held to decide the matter. There will first be a directions hearing, at which a district judge will hear from both parties. Where the conflict between the parents is obvious, some (but not all) courts offer the service of a court welfare officer, who will speak to them together and/or separately and report her findings to the court. If the court does not have a welfare officer available that day, it will consider the conflict between the parents over the arrangements for the children and then order a welfare report to be produced by a welfare officer. A trial date will be set, perhaps three months from the date of the directions hearing.

Orders Concerning Children

Under section 8 of the Children Act 1989, at the start of divorce proceedings various orders regarding children can be sought from the court by a parent. (There is, however, a presumption that where there is no conflict between the parents concerning their children there should be no formal order of the court. In this situation, after divorce responsibility for the children remains with both parents.)

Residency Orders

Formerly known as custody orders, these relate to where the child is going to live. Technically, neither parent is preferred over the other; but if a father has left the former family home and the mother and children remain, it is unlikely that a court will award him residency. Conversely, if it is the mother who has walked out on the family, the father stands an excellent chance of gaining residency. The interest of the child is, as ever, paramount, and the parent remaining in the family home is the one most likely to be able to offer the security of continuity.

Contact Orders

Formerly known as access orders, these state when the parent who has not been awarded residency is going to have contact with the child. Importance is attached by the courts to the children remaining in touch with the parent, and not the other way round as parents often suppose.

Difficult parents may try to deny contact to their former spouse as a form of revenge. This kind of behaviour is actively discouraged by the courts, who will be thoroughly displeased with the offender. If problems of this sort arise, contact centres run by local authorities can be a useful alternative. Here, children can meet their other parent under the eye of social workers.

But parents can get their wishes in subtler, more devious ways: what can happen is that one of them prejudices the child against the other parent so much that contact simply will not work. Because the child's interests are paramount, if the child just does not want to go and see the other parent the court will not force the issue. One of the most galling situations for the 'victim parent' arises if he or she cannot see their child but has to go on paying maintenance.

Contact is about continuity, irrespective of marital break-down, for the sake of the child. The offending parent should realise that continuity and familiarity, with the child still seeing the parent who has left home, are most likely to help the child accept the breakdown of the parents' marriage.

Disputes over Residency and Contact

In both residency and contact disputes the courts may well seek the guidance of a court welfare officer (see above), who interviews each parent in their separate homes and offers the court independent advice. Courts' views are often heavily influenced by these reports, though judges can be impressed by a particular parent in a way that is not highlighted in the welfare report or even missed altogether.

How to Apply for Residency/Contact Orders

Either parent can file a residency application. You fill in the standard court form (see p. 130) and attach a statement setting out why you believe you are the better parent and why the child should come and live with you or continue to do so. You should include any details that will assist the court to come to a decision, though the court will not be interested in what one parent has done to the other unless

- it has clearly had an adverse effect on the child, or
- it demonstrates that the other parent is incapable of being a carer

Copies of this form should be sent both to the court and to the other parent. Similar application forms exist regarding contact. Once filled in, they should be dealt with in the same way.

If you receive a contact or residency application you can then draft a statement in reply. It should:

- set out whatever objections you might have
- suggest who you believe the child should be with, and
- suggest what contact you believe should take place

If one parent is denying the other one contact with their child, it is highly likely that a court welfare officer will be asked to report on:

- the degree of hate, and the reasons for it (known by the courts as the element of acrimony)
- allegations by one parent about the other
- and, most importantly, the interest of the child

Copies of her report will be sent to the court and to both parents.

Once the court office has received the standard forms, you will be given a date for the hearing.

The Hearing

Because the court welfare officer is a busy person she is likely to give evidence to the judge first, so that she can then be released. If one parent disagrees with what the welfare officer has said they should cross-examine, suggest a differing view and wait for her reply. If one parent believes that something vital has been overlooked or that the court welfare officer has been biased, all these thoughts should be put to her in the form of legally phrased questions, like this:

- I suggest to you that you didn't listen to what I said when you came to interview me
- I suggest to you that you are biased

Remember that this stage is for questioning a witness, not for making statements of your own. During the course of the trial both parents will have an opportunity to say whatever they want.

Witnesses

If a parent has witnesses, such as grandparents, aunts or friends of the family, who can say that that parent is capable, they can accompany him or her to court to give evidence. However, court rules insist that any statement these witnesses wish to make verbally in court should first be made in writing and served on the other side at least fourteen days before the hearing. The statement should simply give the name and address of the witness, then go on to state what it is they wish to say. It need not be a sworn affidavit if it relates to children.

8

Other Parties Involved in the Divorce

It is not only the two people immediately involved in a divorce who have an interest in the court's decision. An obvious example is a bank or building society which has provided mortgage facilities on a family home which is now to be sold or its ownership transferred. In such circumstances, interested parties are invited to 'intervene' – in other words, to attend the hearing and put their own points across. Such 'intervenors' might belong to any of the groups described below.

Mortgagees

The consent of the mortgagee (building society, bank or other lender for the purpose of house purchase) is required before the family home can be transferred from one party to another, even if the home has been bought in their joint names. Consent will not usually be withheld unless the lender is worried that the new owner will not be able to afford the repayments. If the intended recipient of the home has a low income, he or she should try to secure a guarantor such as the Department of Social Security to satisfy both the lender and, in due course, the court.

Often the DSS will meet the mortgage repayments for the purchase of a home (though not payments on a mortgage taken out to make improvements), but they will not put this in writing before a court hearing. If they did, anyone trying to obtain a transfer of the family home but lacking adequate funds would be placed in a stronger position.

Additional Owners of the Former Family Home

These are known in legal language as 'beneficial owners besides'. If, for instance, a parent of one half of the divorcing couple had provided the deposit for the purchase of the home and now seeks its return, he or she should 'intervene' so that the court can decide upon their interest.

Creditors

When the marriage breaks down one of the partners might be bankrupt. If so, his trustee in bankruptcy (the person who represents his creditors – those to whom he owes money), might stake a claim on his only asset – the family home – to settle a debt. Alternatively one of the creditors might have obtained judgement against him (a court order that he must meet a debt) and might, again, be seeking to satisfy the judgement by making a claim on his only asset.

A creditor or trustee can seek a sale of the home under Section S30 of the Law of Property Act 1925. The court will then consider the competing claims of the various parties. If the trustee in bankruptcy makes such an application under the Insolvency Act 1986, the court must make an order it thinks is just and reasonable, taking into consideration:

- the interests of the creditors
- the conduct of the former spouse insofar as it might have contributed to the bankruptcy
- the income, if any, of the former spouse
- the needs of the children
- the entire circumstances of the case

If the application is made not less than one year after the bankruptcy the court should allow the creditor's interest to take precedence unless there are exceptional circumstances. These might include the hardship that would be suffered by the wife if she had no home for herself and her children. In this situation the court might place what is called a charge on the property. This would mean that the creditor would be repaid out of the proceeds of the eventual sale of the home, with interest. The court might go on to state that, if there are young children in need of a roof over their heads, the creditor cannot enforce the order until the youngest child has reached the age of eighteen or has ceased full-time education, whichever comes later.

Rented Properties

The law concerning landlord and tenant is extremely complex, and problems encountered here at any stage of your divorce would best be referred to a solicitor who specialises in this area. Briefly, this is the situation.

A contractual tenancy in a rented home can be transferred from a tenant to a non-tenant, as long as the non-tenant is a party to the divorce proceedings. If the contractual tenancy is also a protected one under the Rent Act 1977 it can be transferred on or after divorce. The other spouse then receives the tenancy without due assignment.

Secure tenancies can be assigned under the Housing Act 1985. However, if the lease contained a clause preventing assignment the court is unlikely to permit the transfer.

The landlord, be it a local authority or a private person, must be advised of the probable transfer and his wishes must be known at the time of the court hearing; a letter will be enough. If the landlord withholds consent to a transfer with good reason, the court is unlikely to go against his wishes.

Under the Rent Act 1977 a statutory tenancy exists whereby, when a protected fixed term or periodic tenancy comes to its end, the tenant staying on can do so on the same terms as his former contractual tenancy. As the tenancy is deemed to be by personal occupation and not a right in property, a transfer can only be sought under section 7 Schedule I to the Matrimonial Homes Act 1983. The tenancy must still exist at the time of the application. A sole tenant's wife will not lose her right of occupation if she remains in the former home after the husband has left, but will do so when decree absolute is pronounced.

Assured tenancies (those not subject to the Rent Act 1977) can be transferred on divorce under section S24 of the

Matrimonial Causes Act 1973 and under section 7 Schedule I of the Matrimonial Homes Act 1983. Once more, the wife of an assured tenant will still have rights of occupation if her husband leaves, but these rights disappear at the stage of decree absolute.

9
Divorce and the Tax Man

Income Tax

A married man living with his wife for even part of the year
is entitled to the married couple's allowance for that tax year.
Once divorced, however, a husband and wife are treated as
single individuals for income tax purposes.

Children

After divorce, the parent who is the main carer of a child,
even where there is a joint residency order (see p. 129), is
entitled to single parent assessment. The child in question
must be:

- under sixteen at the beginning of the assessment period, or
- in full-time education, or
- eighteen and maintained by that parent for all or part of
  the relevant tax year

The recipient of maintenance payments has to pay tax on
them.

Tax Relief on Mortgages

Paying mortgage instalments on a property entitles the home
owner to tax relief, which is usually done through the MIRAS
scheme (mortgage interest relief at source). All this means is
that the amount payable is reduced in the first place, so that
the home owner does not have to claim tax relief later.

A court cannot force one ex-spouse to pay the other's
mortgage even though that is what has been laid down.

However, if the court believes the payer can afford the other side's mortgage but is not paying it, it will simply increase the maintenance payment.

As the payer is paying the recipient and not the building society directly, the payer is not entitled to MIRAS. But since the recipient will be using this money to make direct payments on a mortgage in her name, she can seek MIRAS on her own taxable income.

Sometimes the court awards each member of the divorcing couple a percentage of the family home. If, say, the husband wishes to buy out the wife's percentage and raises a loan to do so, he is eligible for tax relief on the interest.

Capital Gains Tax

CGT is a tax payable when you dispose of assets and make a profit, though the first few thousand pounds' worth of profit are always exempt. However, no CGT is charged when husbands and wives dispose of assets between each other.

Homes are treated slightly differently from other assets. No CGT is payable on any profit made when you sell your sole or main residence. Someone who owns more than one property can decide which should be regarded as his main residence for tax purposes. The property selected should have been occupied by him throughout the time of his ownership.

Ex-spouses are considered to be separate individuals for CGT purposes, but again the former family home is an exception. If the home is transferred from one partner to the other after divorce, no capital gains tax is payable as long as the transfer forms part of a court order relating to long-term maintenance (ancillary relief).

When judicially separated or divorced husbands and wives transfer the former family home from one to the other, the spouse who is making the transfer is said for CGT purposes to have remained in occupation until the day of transfer. This ensures that the whole gain (assuming there is one) remains exempt.

The spouse receiving the transfer must have remained in occupation of the property as her main residence. Before the transfer, the other spouse should have chosen any other home as his main residence.

In general, to help divorcing husbands and wives avoid CGT on the former family home there is a two-year moratorium during which gains are exempt. For instance, if the court orders the sale of the home and the husband, say, pays the wife a lump sum out of the proceeds, he will not be liable for CGT provided the sale takes place within two years of his leaving the home and provided that the wife is still occupying the home.

Again, where the home was bought in joint names, the person who is not the occupier will gain exemption on her share of the proceeds as long as the property is sold within two years of her leaving the home. Whichever former partner is still occupying the home at the time of sale is automatically exempt from CGT.

Where a home is transferred into joint names and its sale is deferred beyond the two-year period described above, the partner who does not remain in occupation may find himself liable to CGT on his share of the proceeds. Similarly, where the wife, for instance, now has the home in her sole name but the court has awarded the husband a certain percentage of the proceeds of its eventual sale, he may have to pay CGT.

CGT can be complex, so it is best to consult an accountant if you have any doubts or worries.

Inheritance Tax

This is a tax that has to be paid when you inherit property on someone's death. Transfers between husband and wife are not liable for inheritance tax, although this exemption is lost when you get divorced. There are, however, certain exceptions. These include the payment of maintenance from one party to the other or to a child of either of them.

Transfers of money are also not liable to inheritance tax since they are known in legal terms as transactions 'at arm's length which are not intended to confer any gratuitous benefit'. The Inland Revenue allows such transactions to be exempt.

The position regarding jointly owned homes can be complicated, and to avoid paying inheritance tax unnecessarily it is worthwhile consulting a solicitor or accountant.

10

Failure to Pay Maintenance

What to Do if You Don't Get Your Maintenance Payment

Where a maintenance order is not complied with – in other words, the husband or father refuses to pay up – various enforcement procedures are available. However, no court will order him to pay maintenance if events that have occurred since the original order was made mean that he no longer has any assets or available income.

To help you deal with non-payment, should it arise, register the order in the magistrates' court (unless it was made in the family proceedings court). Take a copy of the original order to the court counter; the court now becomes the recipient of the payments in the first instance and will hand each one on to the mother.

If you make a complaint that the payments are in arrears, the court will have a hearing to investigate the means of the father or husband who has failed to pay. Often courts suggest payment by instalments to deal with the arrears. However, if arrears have mounted up the court might simply wipe the slate clean (called remitting the arrears) rather than have them continue as a millstone around the father's neck. Obviously it is best to make your complaint before this situation is reached.

Various other methods of obtaining money are described below.

Attachment of Earnings

An order for what is known as attachment of earnings can be sought in both the magistrates' court and the divorce court.

What it means is that the employer of the man owing the maintenance will deduct this money at source, before he receives his wages or salary. A cheque is immediately sent to the court and then handed over to the mother or wife.

The exact sum sought each month/week must be stated, as well as the sum below which his earnings cannot reasonably fall. It would not make sense for a working father to be living below the poverty line simply to keep up the attachment of earnings order.

The working father or husband has a duty to inform the court if he changes his job.

Judgement Summons

An application for a judgement summons can be brought in the county court. As in the magistrates' court, there will be a hearing on the father/husband's means before an order, probably again by instalments, is made.

Seizure of Assets

An application can be brought in the county court for what is known legally as a writ of fieri facias. This means that the father/husband's goods can be seized and sold to pay off the debt.

Payment from a Third Party

If a third party owes money to the father or husband, an application can be brought in the county court requiring that person to pay the money directly to the mother. This is known as a garnishee order.

Charging Order

Debts can be 'charged' upon the assets of the father/husband, especially any home or land in his name. The mother's interest can be registered at the local Land Registry office to prevent the property being sold without her consent. If and when it is sold, any debt owing to her will come from the proceeds.

Where to Go for Help

Here is a selection of useful organisations; some of them deal with obvious and direct problems, while others provide more general services.

Asian Family Counselling Service 01274 720486
Association of Separated and Divorced Catholics 0171–371 8253
British Association of Counsellors 01788 778328/9
Capital Radio 0171–388 7575
Catholic Marriage Advisory Service 0171–727 0141
Catholic Marriage Guidance Council 0181–371 1341
Child Poverty Action Group 0171–253 3406
Chiswick Family Rescue 0171–995 4430
Citizens' Advice Bureaux (see your local telephone directory)
Family Mediators Association 0117 9500140
Families Need Fathers 0181–886 0970
Gingerbread 0171–240 0953 (and see your local telephone directory). Support and advice for one-parent families
Jewish Marriage Guidance Council 0181–203 6311
Jewish Mediation Service 0171–636 9380
Joint Council for the Welfare of Immigrants 0171–251 8706
Mediation in Divorce 0181–891 6860
National Council for the Divorced and Separated Trust 0114 2726331
National Council for Voluntary Organisations 0171–713 6161
National Family Conciliation Council (about to be renamed National Association of Family Mediation and Conciliation Services, or Family Mediation for short) 01793 514055. The umbrella organisation for family conciliation services
National Federation of Solo Clubs 0121–236 2879
National Foster Care Association 0171–828 6266

National Stepfamily Association 01223 460313
Nexus 0181–359 7656
One Parent Families 0181–267 1361
RELATE (formerly Marriage Guidance Council) 01788 573241
Samaritans 01753 32713 (see also your local telephone directory)
Shelter 0171–2543 0202. Round-the-clock help with all kinds of housing problems
Solicitors Family Law Association 01689 850 227
Westminster Pastoral Foundation 0171–937 6956
Women's Aid Federation 0171–251 6537
Women's Aid National Office 0117 9428368

Lawyers, Costs and Legal Aid

This is a handbook designed to help you conduct your own divorce. But having read it, you may decide that you would rather someone else did the work. In any case, as pointed out in the preceding chapters, certain aspects of divorce (in particular the financial settlement) are quite complex and you might actually be doing yourself a service if at this stage you consulted a solicitor. But what might it all cost?

Costs

Legal costs spiral upwards with ease. It is easy for the petitioner to lose track of them, since no payment may necessarily be requested during the course of the divorce proceedings.

If a petitioner telephones a solicitor, for instance, that call will be logged and the solicitor's time charged for. VAT is chargeable on top. Clearly it makes sense to ask about rates before committing yourself.

Never forget, either, that work is done, and has to be paid for, that does not necessarily involve you directly – interviewing witnesses, for instance, and attendance at court. If a petitioner has a conference with counsel (the barrister instructed by the solicitor to handle the case), that too will be charged for. If the couple's bank statements or other financial documents are complicated, it is in the petitioner's own interest to peruse them in detail because if counsel has to do it it will take time and cost money. Remember: time is of the essence.

Legal Aid

Don't be taken in by what you may have heard or read about legal aid. It is not necessarily free, and there are strict guidelines concerning who is and is not entitled to it. There are two stages: what is known as the green form scheme, and full legal aid.

Full Legal Aid

In order to qualify for an extension to legal aid, the applicant must have only a limited amount of income and/or capital. Full cover allows you to have a solicitor and a barrister on your case, though the system is not entirely a free one and drawbacks exist. You should have disposable income of no less than about £44 per week to qualify for legal aid without a contribution. However, a figure over that amount could still allow the applicant a legal aid certificate, if he were to contribute to the legal aid granted. Consideration for legal aid will depend upon expenses such as rent, mortgage, travel to work, dependents and the like.

If in due course the applicant, on order of the court, obtains the family home or a part of the net proceeds of sale (equity), the cost of legal aid will be clawed back. The Legal Aid board will fix a charge in its favour on the family home. When the house is sold, it will then claw back whatever is owing to it plus interest since the time of the order.

If the applicant gets a lump sum as a result of a court order, the charge will eat it up if it is over a certain amount. The only exception is if it is sufficiently large to be used or put towards the purchase of a home: this intended use must be stated in the court order, and the court is likely to do so if there are children to be housed. If this occurs, the charge will be deferred until the home is sold.

If you receive no more than £2,500 you will not pay back legal aid. If you receive more than this you might still get legal aid, but you could be required to contribute to your legal aid certificate by paying back whatever you recover or preserve that is more than £2,500.

Solicitors

As mentioned above, different firms of solicitors, like barristers, are likely to charge different rates once the fixed-rate stage is past. 'High Street' firms are less expensive than their counterparts in major towns and cities. This is because their overheads in terms of rent, council tax and so on are likely to be less.

Most 'High Street' firms will take legal aid clients. Big city firms are highly likely to offer no advice to clients on legal aid.

Types of Courts and Their Responsibilities

Courts

Can deal with applications concerning, among other topics:

- parental responsibility
- residence
- contact
- specific issues
- prohibited steps orders
- maintenance and separation orders
- injunctions regarding domestic violence in connection with married/unmarried persons
- payment of lump sums up to £1000 to a spouse/child in family proceedings

Difficult cases regarding children can be sent by the family proceedings court to higher courts.

The majority of appeals on family matters are dealt with by the Family Division of the High Court.

County Court

Can deal with all the matters mentioned above, plus:

- divorce
- nullity cases
- judicial separation
- property issues
- lump sum payments
- costs

Appeals from judges of the county court go to the Court of Appeal. Appeals from district judges go mostly to the county court judge.

High Court (Family Division)

Can deal with any of the matters sent to it by the lower courts.

Court of Appeal

Can deal with cases referred to it by the lower court on a matter of law only.

House of Lords

Can deal with cases referred to it by the lower court on a matter of law only.

Choosing a Court

The family proceedings court is the easiest and cheapest court in which to make applications, but it only has power to award lump sums up to £1000. Therefore if the financial provision you are seeking includes a family home and savings you must go to the county court. If you have started financial application in the county court and then want to bring a residency application, it is sensible to begin that in the same county court so that everything is tied up in one place.

List of Divorce County Courts

Aberystwyth
Accrington
Aldershot and Farnham
Altrincham
Andover
Barnet
Barnsley
Barnstaple
Barrow-in-Furness
Basingstoke
Bath

Bedford
Birkenhead
Birmingham
Bishop Auckland
Blackburn
Blackpool
Blackwood
Bodmin
Bolton
Boston

Bow (London)
Bradford
Brentford
Bridgend
Bridgwater
Brighton
Bristol
Bromley
Burnley
Burton-on-Trent
Bury
Bury St Edmunds
Caernarfon
Camborne and Redruth
Cambridge
Canterbury
Cardiff
Carlisle
Carmarthen
Chelmsford
Chester
Chesterfield
Chichester
Chippenham
Chorley
Colchester
Consett
Coventry
Crewe
Croydon
Darlington
Derby
Dewsbury
Dolgellau
Doncaster
Dudley
Durham
Eastbourne
Edmonton (London)
Epsom
Exeter

Gateshead
Gloucester
Great Grimsby
Guildford
Halifax
Harlow
Harrogate
Hartlepool
Hastings
Haverfordwest
Hereford
Hitchin
Horsham
Huddersfield
Hull (Kingston-upon-Hull)
Ilford
Ipswich
Keighley
Kendal
King's Lynn
Kingston-upon-Thames
Lancaster
Leeds
Leicester
Leigh
Lincoln
Liverpool
Llanelli
Llangefni
London (Bow, Edmonton,
    Wandsworth, Willesden)
Lowestoft
Luton
Macclesfield
Maidstone
Manchester
Mansfield
Medway (Kent)
Merthyr Tydfil
Milton Keynes
Neath and Port Talbot

Nelson
Newcastle-upon-Tyne
Newport (Gwent)
Newport (Isle of Wight)
Northampton
North Shields
Norwich
Nottingham
Oldham
Oxford
Penrith
Peterborough
Plymouth
Pontefract
Pontypridd
Portsmouth
Preston
Rawtenstall
Reading
Reigate
Rhyl
Rochdale
Romford
Rotherham
Runcorn
St Helens
Salford
Salisbury
Scarborough
Scunthorpe
Sheffield
Shrewsbury
Skipton
Slough
Southampton
Southend
Southport
South Shields
Stafford
Staines

Stockport
Stockton-on-Tees
Stoke-on-Trent
Sunderland
Swansea
Swindon
Tameside
Taunton
Teesside
Telford
Thanet (Kent)
Trowbridge
Truro
Tunbridge Wells
Uxbridge
Wakefield
Walsall
Wandsworth (London)
Warrington
Watford
Welshpool and Newtown
West Bromwich
Weston-super-Mare
Weymouth
Whitehaven
Wigan
Willesden (London)
Winchester
Wolverhampton
Worcester
Workington
Worthing
Wrexham
Yeovil
York

Principal Registry
Somerset House
London WC2R 1LP

Court Orders: Appeals and Variations

Appealing Against a Court Order

An order made by a district judge can be appealed against, but only with good reason. It would not be fair to suggest that you could handle an appeal without professional assistance: it makes better sense to instruct a solicitor. However, the appeal process is outlined here so that the various stages will not be totally unfamiliar.

First, an application called a notice of appeal, together with the reasons why the order is being appealed against (the grounds for the appeal) must be served upon the other side and filed at the court.

The appeal is heard before the judge, and simply consists of a rehearing of the case. Any new or recent evidence not presents to the previous court can be placed before the appeal court.

A further level of appeal is possible, to the Court of Appeal. But this can only be made on a point of law – if it is alleged that a judge has not applied a statute properly. Appeals are often sought on the ground that by giving a favourable judgement to the other party a judge has failed to use his discretion properly.

Setting Aside a Court Order

If you want an order of the court to be set aside, you fill in a preliminary application and send it to the court in the usual way. There is no time limit, though the longer you wait the more difficult it may be to obtain permission (leave) to make the application to set the order aside. The power to grant or reject this permission lies with the judge.

There are many reasons why you might seek to set an order aside. Often the two parties in a divorce are not full and frank when disclosing documents: a petitioner wife, for instance, might discover after the court hearing and judgement that the respondent owns far more assets than he previously revealed. Had the court known about these additional assets, it would have made a different order.

Where property is concerned, if a house falls or rises substantially in value, or was wrongly valued through some genuine error, this could change the basis of an order. Say, for instance, a judge believed a house was worth £100,000 and it then sold for £150,000, or vice versa, this would affect a previous court order.

As a rule courts dislike setting aside an order where events following its issue might be said to have changed the basis on which it was originally made. The subsequent occurrence must be very grave, or the courts will simply refuse the application and the order will have to stand.

Varying a Court Order

If you wish to vary an order, you must give notice to the other side by means of an ordinary court form of notice; leave is not required. The respondent should receive his copy of the application within four days of your filing it at the court.

The applicant usually files an affidavit setting out the reasons for bringing the application. If the respondent is willing, an application can be made with the consent of both parties. The court will look again at the original circumstances and at those which are relevant to the application for variation.

Orders that can be varied are:

- periodical payments and secured periodical payment orders
- lump sum instalment order payments
- settlement of property or variation of settlement
- sale of property orders

Orders can also be discharged and suspended, while arrears of maintenance can be remitted – that is, wiped clean. But whilst you can apply for an extension of the time limit for the making of periodical payments, the court can pre-empt this by including in the order a direction that no such application may be made.

It is not possible to vary a periodical payments order by making a property adjustment order or lump sum order. However, a lump sum variation can be made for a child of the family and a maintenance order can be discharged if there is an understanding to make a capital lump sum payment instead. Orders for lump sums can be varied where the sum was to be paid in instalments.

Any variation can be postponed or backdated. Applications to suspend or discharge orders should be made to the court that made the order in the first place.

Where an order has been made for the sale of a house at a future date, either party can seek to have the property sold if the order has not been complied with. It is up to the court to decide whether the application should be granted.

Documents Used in Divorce Proceedings

Documents Used in Divorce Procedures

Court Forms

Court forms are simply documents that have been standardised to make life easier for parties to a divorce regarding whatever applications or defences they may be making. These documents can be picked up at court counters and form part of the ordinary procedure for divorce and are, as yet, the most up-to-date forms available.

Enclosed are examples of the various forms that are usually required in the course of the divorce process though they are, by no means, every document relating to the divorce procedure.

It is hoped that they come across as self-explanatory. The financial forms request the party to simply answer the individual questions posed as to income and expenditure, savings, mortgages, pensions and otherwise, so financial information is collated easily and speedily.

Where the financial aspect of the parties is straightforward in that they are employed, taxed P.A.Y.E. and have savings that are easily located, the standard court form will probably suffice as there will be no need to swear other affidavits regarding financial means, unless of course there are going to be allegations of misappropriation of assets and the like.

Here are the forms:

1

IN THE LONDON COUNTY COURT   NUMBER:

BETWEEN: RENE MARKS PETITIONER

AND

JACK MARKS RESPONDENT

PETITION OF DIVORCE

1. On the 10th of July 1975 the Petitioner, Rene Marks was lawfully married to Jack Marks (hereinafter called the Respondent) at St Adolf's Church, in the Parish of Calder in the County of London.

2. The Petitioner and Respondent last lived together at Hilltops, Lampstead, the County of London.

3. The Petitioner is domiciled in England and Wales and is by occupation a Designer and resides at Hilltops, Lampstead, the County of London.

4. There are no children of the family now living except Mark Menelaus who was born on August the 2nd 1978 and is receiving full time education at University College School, London.

5. There are no other proceedings in any court in England or Wales or elsewhere with reference to the marriage, or to any children of the family or between the Petitioner and the Respondent with reference to any property of either or both of them except that on March 2nd 1991 at London County Court the Respondent was ordered to pay maintenance to the Petitioner on behalf of the one child of the family at the rate of £200 per month and residency of the said child was vested in the Petitioner on January 6th 1992.

6. There are no proceedings continuing in any country outside England and Wales which are in respect of the marriage or are capable of affecting its validity or existence.

7. The said marriage has broken down irretrievably.

8. The Respondent has behaved unreasonably and the Petitioner finds it intolerable to live with the Respondent.

10. PARTICULARS

On December 18th 1991 the Respondent returned to the former matrimonial home in a drunken state, he went into the

1

kitchen and grabbed the Petitioner by the throat, pulling her on to the kitchen table and attempted to force her to have intercourse with him. The next day whilst the Petitioner was in the bathroom he entered without invitation and tried to force her to have intercourse on the bathroom's floor without her consent. During this occasion she suffered bruising to her back, her left leg, her right arm and bleeding to her face.

PRAYER

The Petitioner therefore prays:

1. That the said marriage be dissolved.

2. That the residency of Mark Menelaus be vested in the Petitioner.

3. That the Respondent may be ordered to pay the costs of this suit, if defended.

4. That the Petitioner may be granted the following ancillary relief:
    (a) an order for maintenance pending suit
    a periodical payments order
    a secured provision order
    a lump sum order
    (b) a periodical payments order for the child of the family
    a secured provision order for the child of the family
    a lump sum order for the child of the family
    (c) a property adjustment order

Signed Rene Marks

The name and addresses of the persons to be served with this Petition are:

Respondent: Jack Marks, of Black Cottage, Tighgate, in the County of London

The Petitioner's address for service is: C/o Sparks, Candia Way, Lockleigh, the County of London

DATED

ADDRESS all communications to London County Court at

2

IN THE LONDON COUNTY COURT   NUMBER:

BETWEEN: RENE MARKS PETITIONER

AND

JACK MARKS RESPONDENT

The Respondent in answer to the Petition filed in this suit, says as follows;

1. He admits the matters set out in paragraphs one to seven of the Petition.

2. So far as is known to the Respondent no other child now living has been born to the Petitioner during the said marriage.

3. He admits and avers that the said marriage has broken down irretrievably but denies that such breakdown has been caused by his behaviour as alleged or at all.

4. As to paragraph eight of the Petition he denies that he has behaved in such a way that the Petitioner cannot reasonably be expected to live with him. Save as is hereinafter expressly admitted he denies each and every allegation contained in the Particulars stated at paragraph ten.

(a) He denies that he was drunk when he returned to the former matrimonial home on December 18th 1991 and denies that he grabbed the Petitioner by her throat.

(b) He admits that he pulled her on to the kitchen table and attempted to force her to have intercourse with him.

(c) He denies that he entered the bathroom when the Petitioner was within without her due invitation.

(d) He avers that the Petitioner sought to have intercourse upon the floor of the very bathroom with him.

(e) He denies that she suffered any injury whatsoever.

SIGNED

The names and addresses of the persons to be served with this ANSWER are

(insert any name and address of Solicitors of the Petitioner or the address of the Petitioner herself if unrepresented)

The Respondent's address for service is:

Black Cottage, Tighgate, London

3

IN THE LONDON COUNTY COURT   NUMBER:

BETWEEN: RENE MARKS PETITIONER

AND

JACK MARKS RESPONDENT

The Petitioner in REPLY to the Answer filed in this suit, says that:

1. Save in so far as the same consists of admissions she denies each and every allegation contained in the said ANSWER and joins issue with the Respondent thereon.

2. She avers that the Respondent entered the bathroom without her due invitation and that he sought to have intercourse with her upon the bathroom floor.

3. She avers that she suffered injury.

The Petitioner therefore prays:

(1) As before

TO: Jack Marks, Black Cottage, Tighgate, London

4

FAMILY PROCEEDINGS RULES

*Complete and/or delete as appropriate.

If proceeding in a District Registry, delete both headings and insert "In the High Court of Justice, Family Division   District Registry".

IN THE _____

COUNTY COURT*

PRINCIPAL REGISTRY*

No. of Matter

Between...Petitioner

and ....Respondent

(1) Name, address and description

I,(1)

of

make oath and say: -

    1.   That a copy of the Petition bearing date the   day of

           19   filed in these proceedings together with a Notice of

Proceedings and an Acknowledgement of Service

.

was duly served by me on

.

the   in this case at

.

on the   day of   19   by delivering to the said

.

personally a   copy thereof.

(2) In the case of the respondent, insert here the means of knowledge of the identity of the person served, e.g. a photograph or description.

    2.   (2) And I further make oath and say

SWORN at

this   day of   19

Before me

A Commissioner for Oaths/Solicitor

Notice of Application for Decree Nisi to be made Absolute.
(Form M8, Appendix 1, F.P.R. 1991)

FAMILY PROCEEDINGS RULES

Rule 2.49(1)

*Complete and/or delete as appropriate. If proceeding in a District Registry, delete both headings and insert "in the High Court of Justice, Family Division, District Registry".

IN THE—————————— **COUNTY COURT***

PRINCIPAL REGISTRY*

No. of Matter

Between..Petitioner

and ....Respondent

TAKE NOTICE that the Petitioner

applies for the decree nisi pronounced in his (her) favour on the

day of   19   , to be made absolute.

Dated this   day of   19

Signed..
Solicitors for Petitioner

of...

....

Address all communications for the Court to: The Chief Clerk, County Court*..

....

(or to the Principal Registry, Somerset House, Strand, London WC2R 1LP) quoting the number in the top right-hand corner of this form.
The Court Office is open from 10 a.m. till 4 p.m. (4.30 p.m. at the Principal Registry) on Mondays to Fridays only.

5

NOTICE
of Application for Decree Nisi
to be made Absolute

OYEZ The Solicitors' Law Stationery Society Ltd.   1991 Edition
Oyez House, 7 Spa Road, London SE16 3QQ   8.91 F20576

5046842

Divorce 100   • •

6

Notice of intention to Proceed with Application for Ancillary Relief made in Petition or Answer
(No agreed terms) (Form M 13, Appendix 1, FPR 1991).

**FAMILY
PROCEEDINGS
RULES**

Rule 2.58(1)

*Complete
and/or delete
as appropriate.*

*If proceeding in a
District Registry,
delete both
headings and
insert "In the
High Court of
Justice, Family
Division
District
Registry".*

(1) Or
Respondent.

(2) Or answer.

(3) Here set out the
ancillary relief
claimed and
intended to be
proceeded with,
stating the terms of
any agreement as to
the order which the
Court is to be asked
to make.

IN THE————————————————

COUNTY COURT*

PRINCIPAL REGISTRY*

No. of Matter

Between .... Petitioner

and .... Respondent

[and .... Co-Respondent]

The Petitioner (¹)   having applied in his/her

petition (²)   for (³)

(4) Delete if
not applicable.

(5) Delete this
line and insert
the appropriate
address in the
line above if this
application is
not proceeding
in the Principal
Registry.

(6) This
paragraph is
required unless
the parties are
agreed upon the
terms of the
proposed order
or the application
is for a variation
order.

(⁴) TAKE NOTICE that the application will be heard by   the District Judge

in chambers at

on   day, the   day of   ,19   , at   o'clock.

OR

(⁵) Room   , the Principal Registry, Somerset House, Strand, London WC2R 1LP,

on   day, the   day of   ,19   , at   o'clock.

(⁶) TAKE NOTICE [ALSO] that you must send to the District Judge, so as to reach him/her within

28 days after you receive a copy of the affidavit of the Petitioner (or Respondent], an affidavit

giving full particulars of your property and income. You must at the same time send a copy of

your affidavit to [the Solicitor   for] the applicant. A standard form of affidavit may be obtained

from the Court Office.

(⁶) If you wish to allege that the Petitioner (¹)   has property or income, you

should say so in your affidavit.

Dated this   day of   19

Signed...

Solicitors for Petitioner (¹)

of ....

....

Address all communications for the Court to: The Chief Clerk, County Court* ....

(or to the Principal Registry, Somerset House, Strand, London WC2R 1LP) quoting the number in the top right-hand corner of
this form. The Court Office is open from 10 a.m. till 4 p.m. (4.30 p.m. at the Principal Registry) on Mondays to Fridays only.

6

NOTICE
of Intention to proceed with
Application for Ancillary Relief
(No agreed terms)

Statement of information for a consent order.

FAMILY   IN THE ———————————————————————   **COUNTY COURT***
PROCEEDINGS   **PRINCIPAL REGISTRY***
RULES
Rule 2.61
(M.1)   No. of Matter

*Complete
and/or delete
as appropriate.

Between .... Petitioner

and .... Respondent

Duration of marriage:	**Ages of Parties**
	Age of Petitioner: Age of Respondent:
	Age(s) of any minor or dependent child(ren) (i.e. under the age(s) of 18):

Note	**Summary of means**
If the application is only for an order for interim periodical payments or variation of an order for periodical payments then only the information required under 'net income' need be given.	Give as the date of the statement the approximate amount or value of capital resources and net income of Petitioner and Respondent and, where relevant, of minor child(ren) of the family. State also the net equity in any property concerned and the effect of its proposed distribution.

	Capital resources (less any unpaid mortgage or charge)	Net income
Petitioner		
Respondent		
Child(ren)		

[P.T.O.

7

Where the parties are to live.

Give details of what arrangements are intended for the accommodation of each of the parties and any minor child(ren) of the family.

Marital plans.

Please tick a box.

	Petitioner	Respondent	
	☐	☐	has no present intention to marry or co-habit
	☐	☐	has remarried
	☐	☐	intends to marry
	☐	☐	intends to co-habit with another person

Note	**Notice to mortgagee.**
To be answered by the applicant where the terms of the order provide for a transfer of property.	Has any and every mortgagee of the property been served with notice of the application?

Yes ☐   No ☐

Has any objection to such a transfer been made by any mortgagee within 14 days from the date of service?

Yes ☐   No ☐

Other information.   Give details of any other especially significant matters.

Signatures

(Signed) ....Date.. (Solicitor for the) Petitioner

(Signed) ....Date.. (Solicitor for the) Respondent

Address all communications for the Court to: The Chief Clerk, County Court* ....

(or to the Principal Registry, Somerset House, Strand, London WC2R 1LP) quoting the number in the top right-hand corner of this form. This Court Office is open from 10 a.m. till 4 p.m. (4.30 p.m. at the Principal Registry) on Mondays to Fridays only.

OYEZ The Solicitors' Law Stationery Society Ltd., Oyez House, 7 Spa Road, London SE16 3QQ   1991 Edition
12 91 F20570

Divorce 109   5046930
• •

No.   of 19

DIVORCE REGISTRY

Between

          Petitioner

and

          Respondent

and

          Co-Respondent

Affidavit of means of

Date of swearing:

Solicitors for the

D635

8

Affidavit of Means

*Complete and/or
delete as appropriate.
If proceeding in a
District Registry,
delete both headings
and insert "In the High
Court of Justice, Family
Division,
District Registry".*

IN THE ——————

No. of matter ....

COUNTY COURT*

PRINCIPAL REGISTRY*

Between   Petitioner

and   Respondent

and   Co-Respondent

I

of

**make oath and say that the answers to the questions below are true to the best of my knowledge
information and belief and that they are a full and accurate statement of my means.
Save as set out in the said answers I have no capital or income.**

(1) What is your present occupation?
If you are not now employed, give
details of your last employment and
any trade or professional qualifications.

(2) What is your current gross income from: —
   (a)   your employment, trade or profession

        (i) normal   per year (month) (week)

        (ii) overtime or other special receipts   per year (month) (week)

   (b)   pension or annuities

   (c)   interest on bank or savings deposits

   (d)   building society interest

   (e)   dividends

   (f)   any other source
   *(So far as possible show all receipts of the same period of time: i.e.
   give all weekly, all monthly or all annual amounts. Show all receipts
   as gross amounts before deduction of tax where possible: where
   not possible, indicate that the amount shown is the net amount
   received.)*
   Do you receive any benefits in kind, such as free accommodation,
   use of car, etc.? If so, give details.

(3) What National Insurance contributions are paid by you?   per week

(4) Are there any, and if so what, other expenses, which are necessary
to enable you to earn the income set out above?

(5) (a)   What was your gross taxable income during the last complete
        tax year (6 April to 5 April) from your employment, trade or
        profession including overtime or other special payments and
        taxable benefits?

   (b)   What was your Income Tax liability during the last complete
        tax year?

   *(Where figures for the last complete tax year are not available, give
   them for the last year for which they are available. In the case of
   fluctuating income give also the figures for two or more preceding
   years.)*

1

(6) What do you claim to be your necessary expenses of providing yourself with a place to live in, such as rent, community charge, water rate, mortgage interest and re-payments, premium on endowment insurance used as collateral, etc.?

(7) What maintenance payments (if any) do you make to or receive from your (former) wife/husband including any payments to or for any child and including school fees?

(8) Are any payments to which question (7) refers made —

    (*a*)   under a Court order (give Court, date and details of order)

    (*b*)   under an enforceable agreement (give date and details)

    (*c*)   voluntarily?

(9) What payments (if any) do you receive from the Department of Social Security by way of supplementary pension or supplementary allowance?   *per week*

(10) What family allowance (if any) do you receive for a child or children?   *per week*

(11) Was the former matrimonial home —

    (*a*)   rented

    (*b*)   owned (i) by you

                 (ii) your (former) husband/wife

                 (iii) jointly by you and your (former) husband/wife?

(12) (*a*)   Is the former matrimonial home still occupied by you or your (former) wife/husband or by both of you?

      (*b*)   If it is owned by you or your (former) husband/wife or by you both jointly, at what do you estimate its present value?

      (*c*)   Is it subject to a mortgage? If so, give details of the mortgage, including the rate of any re-payment, the amount outstanding at the date at which re-payment will be completed.

            If there is any collateral security in the form of an endowment assurance, state the surrender value of the policy.

2

8

(13) Do you own any car(s)?   Yes/No

If yes, what is its (their) make, model and year of manufacture and
what do you estimate its (their) present value?

(14) What other assets do you have, such as cash at bank, savings bank
accounts, premium savings bonds, building society account, stock
and shares, reversionary interests, etc.? (Give details and present
value).

Include any house property owned or in which you have an interest,
jointly held property and articles of substantial value such as
jewellery or furniture.

(15) (*a*)   Apart from any liability set out in the answers to questions (8)
and (12) what other unpaid debts are at present due and
payable by you including hire purchase debts?

Also give particulars of any judgments against you.

(*b*)   Do you have any life or endowment assurance policy other
than any set out in the answers to question (6)? If so, give
details including amount of annual premium and date of
maturity.

(16) (*to be answered only by respondents to applications for financial
provision*)

If a decree absolute has been made, have you re-married?

If a decree has not been pronounced or made absolute, do you
intend to re-marry if one is made?

Do you provide for your wife/husband on re-marriage or will you
provide for your intended wife/husband by way of accommodation,
living expenses or otherwise?

Do you provide for any other person? If so, give particulars.

In either case, has the wife/husband, intended wife/husband or
other person any means?
If so, state briefly what they are.

3

8

(17) Are you a member of any pension or superannuation scheme (other
than State Insurance)?   Yes/No

   (*a*)   give details

   (*b*)   would your (former) husband/wife have been entitled to any
benefits at your death in the absence of a decree absolute?   Yes/No

---

(18) Is, to your knowledge, your husband/wife a member of any such
scheme?   Yes/No/Don't know

If so, do you think you will lose any benefits by reason of a decree
absolute, and if so, what?

---

(19) Is there any other reason which you wish to urge against paying
maintenance or are there any other matters which you wish to raise
in connection with this application?

†SWORN at

this   day of   19
   Before me,

       A Commissioner for Oaths/Solicitor.
       Officer of the Court appointed to take affidavits.

---

†If necessary to continue the answers on the following pages, delete jurat and insert at the end of the answers.

8

Affidavit of means of

Date of swearing:

 The Solicitors' Law Stationery Society Ltd., Oyez House,
7 Spa Road, London SE16 3QQ.   *1991 Edition*
8.91 F20660

Divorce 86

9

IN THE LONDON COUNTY COURT   NUMBER:

BETWEEN: RENE MARKS   PETITIONER

AND

JACK MARKS   RESPONDENT

AFFIDAVIT OF PETITIONER IN SUPPORT OF APPLICATION
FOR ANCILLARY RELIEF

I, Rene Marks, of Hilltops, Lampstead, the Petitioner herein, make oath and say as follows:

1. I make this application in support of my application for full ancillary relief as stated in my petition for Divorce and would ask this honourable court to refer to my Petition for the full background of this matter.

2. The former matrimonial home, Hilltops, Lampstead, was bought in 1980 by the Respondent but is in joint names with a current value of £200,000. There is a mortgage outstanding to the Halifax Building Society in the sum of £50,000 with an associated endowment policy with a value of £15,000.

3. The Respondent is a Company Director and I put him to strict proof of his earnings. Last year I am aware that his accountant filed accounts on his behalf with the Inland Revenue stating that his taxable income after deductions regarding expenses to be £75,000. The Respondent also has two accounts outside the jurisdiction, namely, a Special Reserve Account on Jersey, the value of which I believe was, in January of last year, £300,000 and a further account in Switzerland, the value of which I do not know.

4. I myself work part time as a Lecturer in Adult Education earning in the region of £8,000 per annum. I have no savings other than those stated, registered in the Respondent's sole name, abroad. I have an account in Barclays Bank, the High Street, Lampstead, with a current value of £10,000 whilst the Respondent has a personal account with the Midland Bank, in the same street, to a value regarding which I put him to strict proof.

5. Besides the mortgage repayments, I do not intend to specifically depose to my outgoings other than to say that I have to meet bills for electricity, gas and water that are of a general nature. As the Respondent, I suspect, has vast pension funds, the value of which, once more, I put him to strict proof regarding, I verily ask this honourable court to transfer the former matrimonial home into my sole name and to award me maintenance payment and maintenance to the child of the family, Mark Menelaus, who is to go to University and will therefore be continuing full-time education.

10

IN THE LONDON COUNTY COURT   NUMBER:

BETWEEN: RENE MARKS   PETITIONER

                                   AND

                        JACK MARKS   RESPONDENT

RULE 2.63 QUESTIONNAIRE

THE PETITIONER REQUIRES ANSWERS TO THE FOLLOWING QUESTIONS OF THE RESPONDENT:

1. What Bank accounts exist in the name of the Respondent both in England and overseas and please exhibit associated statement of the last six months regarding each of them.

2. What shares are owned by the Respondent and please exhibit associated share certificates.

3. Please exhibit any pension policy held by the Respondent with likely benefits accruing on any chosen retirement date.

4. Please state the value of the home presently occupied by the Respondent producing expert documentary evidence in respect of it.

Signed.

Statement of Arrangements for Children
(Form M4, Appendix 1 FPR 1991)

FAMILY PROCEEDINGS RULES
Rule 2.2(2)

In the	County Court
Petitioner	
Respondent	
No. of Matter *(always quote this)*	

To the Petitioner

You must complete this form
if you or the respondent have any children   ●   under 16

                     or   ●   over 16 but under 18 if they are at school
                                  or college or are training for a trade,
                                  profession or vocation.

Please use black ink.

Please complete Parts I, II and III.

Before you issue a petition for divorce try to reach agreement with your husband/wife over the proposals for the children's future. There is space for him/her to sign at the end of this form if agreement is reached.

If your husband/wife does not agree with the proposals he/she will have the opportunity at a later stage to state why he/she does not agree and will be able to make his/her own proposals.

You should take or send the completed form, signed by you (and, if agreement is reached, by your husband/wife) together with a copy to the Court when you issue your petition.

Please refer to the explanatory notes issued regarding completion of the prayer of the petition if you are asking the Court to make any order regarding the children.

The Court will only make an order if it considers that an order will be better for the child(ren) than no order.

If you wish to apply for any of the orders which may be available to you under Part I or II of the Children Act 1989 you are advised to see a solicitor.

You should obtain legal advice from a solicitor or, alternatively, from an advice agency. The Law Society administers a national panel of solicitors to represent children and other parties involved in proceedings relating to children. Addresses of solicitors (including panel members) and advice agencies can be obtained from the Yellow Pages and the Solicitors Regional Directory which can be found at Citizens Advice Bureaux, Law Centres and any local library.

To the Respondent

The petitioner has completed Parts I, II and III of this form
which will be sent to the Court at the same time that the divorce petition is filed.

Please read all parts of the form carefully.

If you agree with the arrangements and proposals for the children you should sign Part IV of the form.

Please use black ink. You should return the form to the petitioner, or his/her solicitor.

If you do not agree with all or some of the arrangements or proposals you will be given the opportunity of saying so when the divorce petition is served on you.

11

Part I – Details of the children
Please read the instructions for boxes 1, 2 and 3 before you complete this section

1.   Children of both parties
(Give details only of any children born to you and the Respondent or adopted by you both)

	Forenames	Surname	Date of birth
(i)			
(ii)			
(iii)			
(iv)			
(v)			

2.   Other children of the family
(Give details of any other children treated by both of you as children of the family: for example your own or the Respondent's)

	Forenames	Surname	Date of birth	Relationship to Yourself	Respondent
(i)					
(ii)					
(iii)					
(iv)					
(v)					

3.   Other children who are not children of the family
(Give details of any children born to you or the Respondent that have not been treated as children of the family or adopted by you both)

	Forenames	Surname	Date of birth
(i)			
(ii)			
(iii)			
(iv)			
(v)			

2

Part II – Arrangements for the children of the family

This part of the form must be completed. Give details for each child if arrangements are different. If necessary, continue on another sheet and attach it to this form

4.	**Home details** *(Please tick the appropriate boxes)*	
	(a) The addresses at which the children now live	
	(b) Give details of the number of living rooms, bedrooms, etc. at the addresses in (a)	
	(c) Is the house rented or owned and by whom? Is the rent or any mortgage being regularly paid?	☐ No ☐ Yes
	(d) Give the names of all other persons living with the children including your husband/wife if he/she lives there. State their relationship to the children.	
	(e) Will there be any change in these arrangements?	☐ No ☐ Yes *(please give details)*

3

11

5.	Education and training details *(Please tick the appropriate boxes)*
(a) Give the names of the school, college or place of training attended by each child.	
(b) Do the children have any special educational needs?	☐ No ☐ Yes *(please give details)*
(c) Is the school, college or place of training, fee-paying?	☐ No ☐ Yes *(please give details of how much the fees are per term/year)*
Are fees being regularly paid?	☐ No ☐ Yes *(please give details)*
(d) Will there be any change in these arrangements?	☐ No ☐ Yes *(please give details)*

4

11

6.	**Childcare details** *(Please tick the appropriate boxes)*	
(a)	Which parent looks after the children from day to day? If responsibility is shared, please give details.	
(b)	Does that parent go out to work?	☐ No ☐ Yes *(please give details of his/her hours of work)*
(c)	Does someone look after the children when the parent is not there?	☐ No ☐ Yes *(please give details)*
(d)	Who looks after the children during school holidays?	
(e)	Will there be any change in these arrangements?	☐ No ☐ Yes *(please give details)*

7.	**Maintenance** *(Please tick the appropriate boxes)*	
(a)	Does your husband/wife pay towards the upkeep of the children? If there is another source of maintenance, please specify.	☐ No ☐ Yes *(please give details of how much)*
(b)	Is the payment made under a court order?	☐ No ☐ Yes *(please give details, including the name of the court and case number)*
(c)	Has maintenance for the children been agreed?	☐ No ☐ Yes
	If not, will you be applying for a maintenance order for the children?	☐ No ☐ Yes *(please give details)*

5

11

8.	**Details for contact with the children** *(Please tick the appropriate boxes)*
(a) Do the children see your husband/wife?	☐ No ☐ Yes *(please give details of how often and where)*
(b) Do the children ever stay with your husband/wife?	☐ No ☐ Yes *(please give details of how much)*
(c) Will there be any change to these arrangements? Please give details of the proposed arrangements for contact and residence.	☐ No ☐ Yes *(please give details of how much)*

6

11

9. Details of health *(Please tick the appropriate boxes)*

(a) Are the children generally in good health?

☐ Yes ☐ No *(please give details of any serious disability or chronic illness)*

(b) Do the children have any special health needs?

☐ No ☐ Yes *(please give details of the care needed and how it is to be provided)*

10. Details of care and other court proceedings *(Please tick the appropriate boxes)*

(a) Are the children in the care of a local authority, or under the supervision of a social worker or probation officer?

☐ No ☐ Yes *(please give details including any court proceedings)*

(b) Are any of the children on the Child Protection Register?

☐ No ☐ Yes *(please give details of the local authority and the date of registration)*

(c) Are there or have there been any proceedings in any Court involving the children, for example adoption, custody/residence, access/contact wardship, care, supervision or maintenance?

☐ No ☐ Yes *(please give details and send a copy of any order to the Court)*

7

11

Part III – To the Petitioner

Conciliation

If you and your husband/wife do not agree about the arrangements for the child(ren), would you agree to discuss the matter with a Conciliator and your husband/wife?

☐ No   ☐ Yes

Declaration

I declare that the information I have given is correct and complete to the best of my knowledge.

Signed   (Petitioner)

Date:

Part IV – To the Respondent

I agree with the arrangements and proposals contained in Part I and II of this form.

Signed   (Respondent)

Date:

8

OYEZ The Solicitors' Law Stationery Society Ltd, Oyez House, 7 Spa Road, London SE16 3QQ

1991 Edition
6 92 F22621

5046127

* * * *

Divorce 8

OYEZ

Application for an Order

Form C1

(Children Act 1989)

The Court

The full name(s) of the child(ren)

To be completed by the Court

Date issued

Case number

Child(ren)'s number(s)

1. About you (the Applicant).

State ● *your title, full name, address, telephone number, date of birth and relationship to each child above*
 ● *your solicitor's name, address, reference, telephone, fax and DX numbers.*

2. The child(ren) and the order(s) you are applying for.

For each child state ● *the full name, date of birth and sex*
 ● *the type of order(s) you are applying for (for example, residence order, contact order, supervision order).*

1

[P.T.O.

12

3. **Other cases which concern the child(ren).**

   If there have ever been, or there are pending, any court cases which concern
   - *a child whose name you have put in paragraph 2*
   - *a full, half or step brother or sister of a child whose name you have put in paragraph 2*
   - *a person in this case who is or has been, involved in caring for a child whose name you have put in paragraph 2,*

   please attach a copy of the relevant order and give
   - *the name of the Court*
   - *the name and **panel** address (if known) of the guardian ad litem, if appointed*
   - *the name and contact address (if known) of the court welfare officer, if appointed*
   - *the name and contact address (if known) of the solicitor appointed for the child(ren).*

4. **The Respondent(s).**

   (Appendix 3 Family Proceedings Courts Rules 1991; Schedule 2 Family Proceedings (Children Act 1989) Rules 1991).
   For each Respondent state
   - *the title, full name and address*
   - *the date of birth (if known) or the age*
   - *the relationship to each child.*

5. Others to whom notice is to be given.

(Appendix 3 Family Proceedings Rules 1991; Schedule 2 Family Proceedings Courts (Children Act 1989) Rules 1991).

For each person state   • *the title, full name and address*

   • *the date of birth (if known) or age*

   • *the relationship to each child.*

6. The care of the child(ren).

For each child in paragraph 2 state

• *the child's current address and how long the child has lived there*

• *whether it is the child's usual address and who cares for the child there*

• *the child's relationship to the other children (if any).*

7. Social Services.

For each child in paragraph 2 state

• *whether the child is known to the Social Services. If so, give the name of the social worker and the address of the Social Services Department*

• *whether the child is, or has been, on the Child Protection Register. If so, give the date of registration.*

[P.T.O.

12

8. **The education and health of the child(ren).**
    For each child state ● *the name of the school, college or place of training which the child attends*
    ● *whether the child is in good health. Give details of any serious disabilities or ill health*
    ● *whether the child has any special needs.*

9. **The Parent(s) of the child(ren).**
    For each child state ● *the full name of the child's mother and father*
    ● *whether the parents are, or have been, married to each other*
    ● *whether the parents live together. If so, where*
    ● *whether, to your knowledge, either of the parents have been involved in a Court case concerning a child. If so, give the date and the name of the Court.*

10. **The Family of the child(ren) (other children).**
    For any other child not already mentioned in the family (for example, a brother or a half sister) state
    ● *the full name and address*
    ● *the date of birth (if known) or age*
    ● *the relationship of the child to you.*

12

11.   Other adults.

State   • *the full name, of any other adults (for example, lodgers) who live at the same address as any child named in paragraph 2*
   • *whether they live there all the time*
   • *whether, to your knowledge, the adult has been involved in a Court case concerning a child. If so, give the date and the name of the Court.*

12.   Your reason(s) for applying and any plans for the child(ren).

State briefly your reasons for applying and what you want the Court to order.
   • ***Do not*** *give a full statement if you are applying for an order under Section 8 of Children Act 1989. You may be asked to provide a full statement later.*
   • ***Do not*** *complete this section if this form is accompanied by a prescribed supplement.*

13.   At the Court.

State   • *whether you will need an interpreter at Court (parties are responsible for providing their own). If so, please specify the language*
   • *whether disabled facilities will be needed at Court.*

Signed
(Applicant)   Date

OYEZ The Solicitors' Law Stationery Society Ltd, Oyez House, 7 Spa Road, London SE16 3QQ

1995 Edition
11.94   F28402
5037502
* * *

Children Act —C1

13

Oyez

Supplement for an Application for Financial Provision for a Child or Variation of Financial Provision for a Child

Form C10

(Paragraph 4 Schedule 1 Children Act 1989)

The Court	**To be completed by the Court**
	Date issued
	Case number
The full name(s) of the child(ren)	Child(ren)'s number(s)

1.   About the application.

State whether you are seeking

- *an order for a lump sum; a transfer of property; a settlement of property; periodical payments; secured periodical payments*

or • *a variation of an order for periodical payments; secured periodical payments; payment of a lump sum by instalments.*

Note: *Applications concerning transfer of property, settlement of property or secured periodical payments can only be heard in the High Court or a County Court.*

2.   Previous Court Orders and written agreements.

If a written agreement or Court Order has been made a copy should be attached to this application.

If not available state • *the date*
- *the terms*
- *the parties*
- *the Court.*

[P.T.O.

3. The Child Support Agency.

Assessment for maintenance

State whether the Agency has made an assessment for the maintenance of the child(ren):

☐ Yes ☐ No

If Yes, state whether you are applying for additional child maintenance

- because the Child Support Agency will no longer deal with your claim. You should explain why the Agency will not deal with the claim

or • on top of payments made through the Child Support Agency. You should explain why you need additional maintenance and confirm that the Child Support Agency's assessment is the maximum amount obtainable.

Written agreement for maintenance

State whether there is a written maintenance agreement: ☐ Yes ☐ No

If No, state whether you are applying for payment:

☐ for [a] stepchild[ren]

☐ in addition to child support maintenance already paid under a Child Support Agency assessment

   ☐ to meet expenses arising from the disability of [a] child[ren]

   ☐ to meet expenses incurred by [a] child[ren] in being educated or training for work

   ☐ when either the child[ren] OR the person with care of the child[ren] OR the absent parent of the child[ren] is not habitually resident in the United Kingdom

   ☐ for any other reason *(please specify):*

13

4. About the Order.

State the terms of the Order you ask the Court to make and in particular
- *the amount you would like the Court to order*
- *whether you would like that amount paid weekly or monthly (if you are not applying for a lump sum)*
- *why you require the payments, or would like the Court to vary an existing order.*

5. The collection of payment.

If payments are not to be collected and paid to you by the Child Support Agency, give full details of how you would like the payments collected. Possible ways are:

☐ **Directly to a bank, building society or post office account.**
Give the full name and address, sorting code and the number of the account into which payment is to be made.

☐ **By an attachment of earnings order.**
This is a Court order which is sent to the employer of the person who is to pay.

☐ **If you would like the Court to direct that money is paid in some other way.**
Please say what method you would like and if you do not mind how the money is paid, please say so. The Court will decide how it should be paid.

Signed   Date
(Applicant)

You should now complete a Statement of Means, Form Children Act — C10A

3

Statement of Means
(Schedule 1 Children Act 1989)

Form C10A

The Court	To be completed by the Court
	Date issued
The full name(s) of the child(ren)	Case number
	Child(ren)'s number(s)

Warning—The Court will require to see written evidence of unemployment or sickness; or wage or salary slips, bank statements, and other papers giving details of your means. This evidence should be attached to this form or brought with you when you attend the hearing.

1. **About you.**
   State • *your title, full name, address, telephone number and date of birth*
   • *whether you are married, single or other*
   • *whether you are the Applicant or the Respondent.*

2. **Your Dependants.**
   State for each Dependant • *the Dependant's title, full name and age*
   • *whether the Dependant is a spouse, partner, child or other*
   • *whether the Dependant is wholly or partially financially dependent on you*
   • *whether the Dependant lives with you.*

3. **Your employment.**
   State whether you are employed, self-employed, unemployed or other.
   If you are employed, state • *your employment*
   • *your Employer's name, address and daytime telephone number.*

[P.T.O.

14

4. **Your buildings and land.**
   List all buildings and land you own, whether in your name alone or jointly, stating for each
   - *the address*
   - *the name(s) of the owner(s)*
   - *the current value.*

5. **Your financial assets.**
   List each bank, building society and post office account, stating for each
   - *the name and address where the account is held*
   - *the account number*
   - *the current balance.*

   List all investments and securities (for example, shares, insurance policies) stating for each one the name and quantity and current value. List all pension schemes, stating for each one the scheme name and the Company.

6. **Other possessions of value.**
   List all possessions of value (for example, jewellery, antiques, collectable items), stating for each:
   - *what they are*
   - *the current value.*

2

14

7. Your income.

	State whether Weekly(W) or Monthly(M)
If employed, state your usual take home pay	£
If self employed, state ● your drawings	£
● your gross turnover	£
● your profit after expenses	£
● whether you expect your turnover to increase, decrease or remain the same:	
● the date of the accounts showing the above gross turnover and profit after expenses	Year ending · 19

In all cases, state any of the following which you receive

● Income support	£
● Child benefits	£
● Child Support Agency	£
● Other state benefits (specify source)	£ £ £
● Pension(s) (specify source)	£ £ £
● Contributions from others in the home (total) ● Other income (specify source and amount)	£ £ £ £ £
Total income:	£

8. Court Orders.
Enclose a copy of any order

Court	Case Number	Amount outstanding (£)	Amount of payment (£)	Weekly(W) or Monthly(M)

3

[P.T.O.

14

9.	Your expenses.	Amount of payments	Weekly (W) or Monthly (M)	Total debt	Amount of arrears
	Mortgage 1st				
	2nd				
	Rent				
	Council tax				
	Gas				
	Electricity				
	Telephone				
	Water charges				
	Credit card				
	Loans				
	Storecards				
	HP payments				
	TV rental and licence				
	Mail order				
	Food				
	Clothing				
	Public transport				
	Car expenses				
	School meals				
	Child minding				
	Maintenance				
	Child Support Agency				
	Other payments (give details)				
	Total Payments				

Signed   Date

[Applicant] [Respondent]

OYEZ   The Solicitors' Law Stationery Society Ltd, Oyez House, 7 Spa Road, London SE16 3QQ

1995 Edition
11.94   F28413
5037600
★ ★ ★

Children Act—C10A

Glossary of Legal Terms

Acknowledgement of Service The form that is sent with the petition for the respondent to acknowledge the petition's receipt. When the form is returned, SERVICE is accepted as having been achieved.

Affidavit A written statement, made on oath, containing a version of events, beliefs and opinions which will be relied upon as evidence by the person making the affidavit.

Ancillary Relief Long-term maintenance which comes into effect after decree absolute.

Answer The reply to a divorce petition or CROSS-PETITION.

Application All divorce proceedings and court orders begin with an application: standard forms for filling out are available from the court office.

Calderbank Letter A letter containing a financial offer, written in advance of a final hearing (see p. 45).

In Chambers Almost all divorce proceedings are heard in chambers, in other words in private.

Child of the Family A child who naturally belongs to the husband and wife who are getting divorced, or any other child who has been treated by the two of them as a child of the family.

Clean Break An agreement that the two people who are divorcing will have no further financial dependence on each other.

Conciliation An attempt to obtain agreement between the divorcing couple concerning their children and any other areas of conflict.

Co-respondent The person with whom it is alleged the respondent has committed adultery.

Contact Formerly called access, contact is the visiting right or staying right of either parent to a child of the family; in other words, a right to have contact with that child.

Cross-petition   The reasons for the breakdown of the marriage put forward by the respondent, which will differ from those stated by the petitioner.

Decree Absolute   The final order of the court to dissolve the marriage.

Decree Nisi   The provisional order of the court to dissolve the marriage.

Domicile   A person's permanent home.

Equity   The net proceeds of the sale of the family home, after deduction of estate agent's and solicitor's fees and paying off the remaining mortgage.

Habitual Residence   The place where a person resides 'as of habit' – that is, permanently – for the purposes of the law.

Injunction   A court order to restrain or prevent the recipient from, for example, molesting his wife or entering the family home.

Jurisdiction   A court's authority and the geographical area covered by that authority.

Legal Aid   Payment by the state for legal representation; certain conditions are attached to its availability (see p. 71).

Nullity   A decree stating that a marriage is null and void.

Prohibited Steps Order   An order restricting what a parent may do with a child – preventing the parent, for instance, from taking the child out of the country.

Reply   A response/defence filed by the petitioner in answer to the reply and/or **Cross-petition** of the respondent.

Residency   Formerly known as custody, this refers to a parent having the child of the family permanently with him/her – in other words he or she has the permanent residency of the child. Residency can also be shared, for which purpose an order of shared residency can be made.

Service   The manner in which the parties to the divorce receive the necessary court forms.

Index